Garfield
FAT CAT 3-PACK
VOLUME 1

BY
JIM DAVIS

BALLANTINE BOOKS · NEW YORK

LOOK INSIDE THIS BOOK AND SEE THIS CAT...

- EAT LASAGNA
- CHASE DOGS
- DESTROY A MAILMAN
- LAUGH; CRY, FFFT
- SHRED HIS OWNER
- AND MUCH, MUCH MORE!

A Ballantine Book
Published by The Random House Publishing Group

Published in the United States by Ballantine Books, an imprint of The Random House Publishing Group, a division of Random House, Inc., New York, and simultaneously in Canada by Random House of Canada Limited, Toronto.

www.ballantinebooks.com

Library of Congress Control Number: 2003105484

ISBN 0-345-46455-9

Manufactured in the United States of America

First Colorized Edition: September 2003

9 8 7

Garfield at large

BY: JIM DAVIS

HI, THERE... I'M JON ARBUCKLE. I'M A CARTOONIST, AND THIS IS MY CAT, GARFIELD.
© 1978 PAWS, INC. All Rights Reserved.

JIM DAVIS 6-19
HI, THERE. I'M GARFIELD. I'M A CAT, AND THIS IS MY CARTOONIST, JON.

OUR ONLY THOUGHT IS TO ENTERTAIN YOU.
FEED ME.

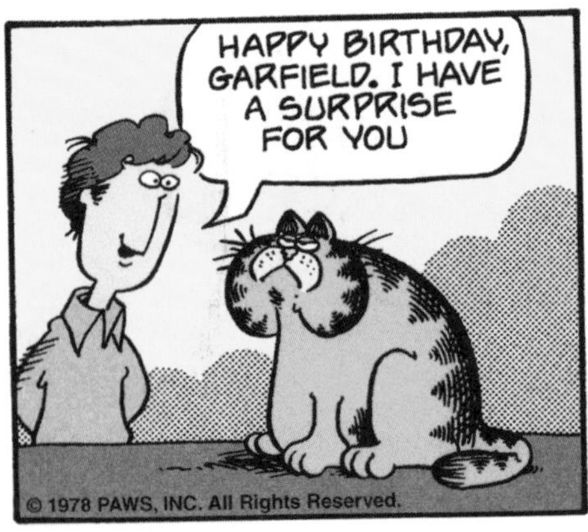
HAPPY BIRTHDAY, GARFIELD. I HAVE A SURPRISE FOR YOU
© 1978 PAWS, INC. All Rights Reserved.

A RUBBER MOUSEY!
6-20

COULD'VE USED A LITTLE SALT...
JIM DAVIS

A MOUSE! GET IT!

GARFIELD! YOU DIDN'T EVEN TRY!
© 1978 PAWS, INC. All Rights Reserved.

SHOW ME A GOOD MOUSER, AND I'LL SHOW YOU A CAT WITH BAD BREATH.
6-21
JIM DAVIS

I'M PUTTING YOU ON A DIET, GARFIELD... HERE'S YOUR DINNER.

WHA...

© 1978 PAWS, INC. All Rights Reserved.
6-22
JIM DAVIS

JIM DAVIS
© 1978 PAWS, INC. All Rights Reserved.
6/23

AHHHHH...

HAPPINESS IS A WARM TELEVISION SET.

SLAP!
© 1978 PAWS, INC. All Rights Reserved.

DON'T BE CRUEL, GARFIELD. PUT THE CATBURGER OUT OF ITS MISERY AND EAT IT.
6/24
JIM DAVIS

GARFIELD®

CATS...

WE CATS ARE INTELLIGENT, SOFT, CUTE...
6-25

FURRY CUDDLY...

PLAYFUL...

DEMURE...

AND MASTERS OF THE HOUSE.
GARFIELD
®
JIM DAVIS

WE CATS LIKE TO SIT IN HIGH PLACES. IT REINFORCES OUR SUPERIORITY.
6-26

HELP
© 1978 PAWS, INC. All Rights Reserved.
JIM DAVIS

6-27

© 1978 PAWS, INC. All Rights Reserved.

JIM DAVIS
GARFIELD, YOU DUMMY.

HERE, GARFIELD, ...BEG.
6/28

EEYOUCH!!
SWIPE!

GROVELING IS NOT ONE OF MY STRONG SUITS.
© 1978 PAWS, INC. All Rights Reserved.
JIM DAVIS

YOU CAN'T DRINK COFFEE, GARFIELD. YOU'LL STUNT YOUR, UH, YOUR...
© 1978 PAWS, INC. All Rights Reserved.

6-29

ONE LUMP, OR TWO?
JIM DAVIS

ALL I EVER DO IS EAT AND SLEEP, EAT AND SLEEP, EAT AND SLEEP.
6-30
GARFIELD

THERE MUST BE MORE TO A CAT'S LIFE THAN THAT.
GARFIELD

BUT, I HOPE NOT.
GARFIELD
© 1978 PAWS, INC. All Rights Reserved.
JIM DAVIS

THIS IS IT, GARFIELD. THE LATE-LATE MOVIE WITH BRIGITTE BARDOT
7/1
© 1978 PAWS, INC. All Rights Reserved.

GOT OUR SODA POP. GOT OUR POPCORN. WE'RE SET

JIM DAVIS
ZZZZZZ
ZZZZZ

GARFIELD®

I'M OUT OF SHAPE.

I THINK I'LL TAKE UP JOGGING.

7-2

PANT
PANT
PANT
PANT

© 1978 PAWS, INC. All Rights Reserved.
WHEW! MADE IT.
GARFIELD
®
JIM DAVIS

© 1978 PAWS, INC. All Rights Reserved.

PURRR

I HATE STATIC ELECTRICITY.
7-3
JIM DAVIS

I REALLY SHOULDN'T EAT THAT FISH...
7-4

© 1978 PAWS, INC. All Rights Reserved.
JIM DAVIS

CALL IT AN ETHNIC WEAKNESS.

ITCH
SCRATCH SCRATCH
7-5
© 1978 PAWS, INC. All Rights Reserved.

SCRATCH! SCRATCH! SCRATCH! SCRATCH!
ITCH
SCRATCH! SCRATCH! SCRATCH! SCRATCH!

AARRRGH!
JIM DAVIS

DEAR GARFIELD:
BELIEVE IT OR NOT, I AM AN UGLY KITTEN! OH, I DO ALL THE THINGS "CUTE" KITTENS DO... PLAY WITH YARN AND SUCH, BUT I DON'T GET ANY ATTENTION. WHAT CAN I DO?
MUD FENCE

DEAR "MUD":
YOU'RE TRYING TOO HARD TO BE CUTE. YOU'LL GET MORE ATTENTION IF YOU JUST BE YOURSELF...

GARFIELD®

STEAK!

BANZAI!

POOMP!

7-9

GARFIELD!
© 1978 PAWS, INC. All Rights Reserved.

HISSS!

®
EVEN A HOUSE CAT HAS TO FORAGE FOR HIMSELF ONCE IN A WHILE
JIM DAVIS

© 1978 PAWS, INC. All Rights Reserved.
HMMMM... A NEW SOFA
7-10

MUCH BETTER
JIM DAVIS

I'M GETTING LAZY. IT WOULD DO ME GOOD TO GET SOME EXERCISE.
© 1978 PAWS, INC. All Rights Reserved.

YAWN

MUCH BETTER
7-11
JIM DAVIS

LOVE A COOKOUT
7-12

MIND IF I SMOKE?
© 1978 PAWS, INC. All Rights Reserved.
JIM DAVIS

NOW HERE'S WHERE LIEUTENANT LACROIX FINDS A SPOT OF BLOOD ON THE BUTLER'S SLEEVE... SO HE FIGURES, "AHA! THIS GUY IS ACTING VERY SUSPIC...

GARFIELD®

© 1978 PAWS, INC. All Rights Reserved.
GARFIELD! BATH TIME!

ZIPPPPP!

GARFIELD?

SCREEEEEEE
JIM DAVIS
7/16

YOU DO WHAT YOU HAVE TO.

THIS IS THE LIFE. I DON'T THINK I'LL EVER GET OUT OF BED AGAIN.
© 1978 PAWS, INC. All Rights Reserved.
7-17

I'M HUNGRY
JIM DAVIS

GOOD NEWS, GARFIELD!

THE ADMINISTRATION SAYS THE RATE OF INFLATION IS GOING DOWN.
© 1978 PAWS, INC. All Rights Reserved.

THAT AND A BUCK-FIFTY WILL GET YOU A CUP OF COFFEE.
7-18
JIM DAVIS

AH, HERE COMES THE MAILMAN.

7-19

WHY SHOULD DOGS HAVE ALL THE FUN?
© 1978 PAWS, INC. All Rights Reserved.
JIM DAVIS

OH BOY, OH BOY. TODAY IS THURSDAY, AND THAT'S LASAGNA DAY.
7-20

CAT FOOD!
GARFIELD

© 1978 PAWS, INC. All Rights Reserved.
GARFIELD
JIM DAVIS

TICKLE, TICKLE,
© 1978 PAWS, INC. All Rights Reserved.

TICKLE-TICKLE-TICKLE!

I THINK I'M GOING TO THROW UP
7-21
JIM DAVIS

YAWN
7-22

CRICK!
© 1978 PAWS, INC. All Rights Reserved.
JIM DAVIS

HELLO, DOCTOR?...
MY CAT'S STUCK IN A STRETCH.

GARFIELD®

© 1978 PAWS, INC. All Rights Reserved.
7/23

BEWARE OF CAT!

SLURP
MUNCH
SMACK
© 1978 PAWS, INC. All Rights Reserved.

GARFIELD, YOU'RE A FAT, ARROGANT, LAZY PIG.

WELL, EXCUUUUUUSE ME!
JIM DAVIS
7-24

7-25
JIM DAVIS

© 1978 PAWS, INC. All Rights Reserved.

GARFIELD, CUT THAT OUT!

SQUIRT!
7-26
JIM DAVIS

CHUNK
CHUNK
CHUNK
CHUNK
CHUNK
CHUNK
CHUNK
CHUNK

GARFIELD, YOU SHOULD REALLY LEARN TO CONTROL YOUR TEMPER
© 1978 PAWS, INC. All Rights Reserved.

© 1978 PAWS, INC. All Rights Reserved.

NOW WHERE COULD MY PIPE BE?

GARFIELD!!
7-27
JIM DAVIS

POOK!
© 1978 PAWS, INC. All Rights Reserved.
7-28

JIM DAVIS

HEH, HEH, HEH.
M-I-C
7-29

A CAT WHO LIKES MICKEY MOUSE
K-E-Y

SHAKE IT, ANNETTE
© 1978 PAWS, INC. All Rights Reserved.
JIM DAVIS

GARFIELD®

© 1978 PAWS, INC. All Rights Reserved.
7-30

JIM DAVIS

DON'T TRY LOOKING CUTE AT ME, GARFIELD. YOU STILL CAN'T HAVE ANY OF MY STEAK.

GIRL SCOUTS LIKE ME
JIM DAVIS

B-B-B-B-B-B
7-31
© 1978 PAWS, INC. All Rights Reserved.

AAAAAAAA
I AMUSE THEM

SCRATCH
SCRATCH
SCRATCH
SCRATCH
© 1978 PAWS, INC. All Rights Reserved.
8-1

OOPS. I GOT A SCRATCH ON JON'S FAVORITE CHAIR

MAYBE HE WON'T NOTICE
JIM DAVIS

ONE LAST OLIVE
© 1978 PAWS, INC. All Rights Reserved.
8-2

CLUNK
CLUNK
CLUNK
JIM DAVIS

© 1978 PAWS, INC. All Rights Reserved.
JIM DAVIS
8-3

SSSSSS

ONE WORD ABOUT CURIOSITY KILLING THE CAT, AND I'LL BREAK YOUR FACE.

I HATE TELEVISION COMMERCIALS
8-4

THEY'RE TOO LONG TO SIT THROUGH...

-AND THEY'RE TOO SHORT FOR A TRIP TO THE SANDBOX!
© 1978 PAWS, INC. All Rights Reserved.
JIM DAVIS

© 1978 PAWS, INC. All Rights Reserved.

NEVER TRUST A SMILING CAT
8-5
JIM DAVIS

GARFIELD®

NOTHING TO DO TODAY BUT HANG ON THE SCREEN DOOR...

I'M BORED

BORED, BORED, BORED, BORED.
JIM DAVIS

BORED, BORED, BORED, BORED, BORED, BORED, BORED, BORED, BORED.

I WISH SOMETHING WOULD HAPPEN
© 1978 PAWS, INC. All Rights Reserved.

GARFIELD! LUNCH TIME !!!
SLAM!

I'M IN PAIN... PAIN, PAIN, PAIN, PAIN.
8-6

DING
DONG

LYMAN
JON

I'M COLD. I'M HUNGRY. I'M WEAK. TAKE ME IN!
8-7
JIM DAVIS
© 1978 PAWS, INC. All Rights Reserved.
SURE, LYMAN. YOU KNOW MY HOME IS YOUR HOME.
AND MY SANDBOX IS OFF-LIMITS.

IS THAT ALL YOU HAVE, THE ONE SUITCASE?
NOT EXACTLY

HERE BOY!

© 1978 PAWS, INC. All Rights Reserved.
OH, LAWSEY, LAWSEY, LAWSEY.
8-8
JIM DAVIS

COME ON, GARFIELD. SNAP OUT OF THIS DEEP BLUE FUNK. SO WHAT IF A DOG MOVED IN...

YOU CAN HANDLE IT. CHEER UP.

8-9
© 1978 PAWS, INC. All Rights Reserved.

TAKE ME NOW, LORD!
JIM DAVIS

WHAT'S YOUR DOG'S NAME?
ODIE
8-10
© 1978 PAWS, INC. All Rights Reserved.

ODIE... A DOG NAMED ODIE...

A BLIMP NAMED HINDENBURG.
A SHIP NAMED TITANIC.
A CAR NAMED EDSEL.
JIM DAVIS

© 1978 PAWS, INC. All Rights Reserved.

CRASH!

TEN BILLION DOGS IN THIS WORLD, AND I GET TWEEDLDEE, THE WONDER DUMMY.
8-11
JIM DAVIS

WOOF!
© 1978 PAWS, INC. All Rights Reserved.
8-12

BARK!

YIP!
YIP!
YIP!
YIP!
JIM DAVIS

GARFIELD®

POOR ME.

SIGH...A BIG, VICIOUS, BRUTE OF A DOG HAS MOVED INTO MY HOME...

GRAB!

WHAP
WHAP
WHAP
WHAP
WHAP
WHAP
WHAP

DRIBBLE
DRIBBLE
DRIBBLE
© 1978 PAWS, INC. All Rights Reserved.
8-13
®

PUNT

HOW WILL I EVER SURVIVE?
JIM DAVIS

DOES IT HURT TO RUB A CAT THE WRONG WAY ?
I DON'T KNOW
© 1978 PAWS, INC. All Rights Reserved.
8-14

ROWRRRRR!!!

YUP
JIM DAVIS

ODIE! LOOK WHAT YOU DID ON THE FLOOR!
8-15

YIP! YIP! YIP!
NO! NO! NO! NO! NO! NO!
WHAP! WHAP! WHAP!

THEY SHOULD'VE NAMED HIM "SPOT"
© 1978 PAWS, INC. All Rights Reserved.
JIM DAVIS

LYMAN, YOU GOTTA HOUSEBREAK ODIE
HOW?
© 1978 PAWS, INC. All Rights Reserved.
8-16

SWAT HIM WITH SOMETHING
WITH WHAT ?

JIM DAVIS

© 1978 PAWS, INC. All Rights Reserved.
8-17

PAT
PAT
PAT
PAT

JIM DAVIS

I THINK I'LL PUT THAT DOG'S LIGHTS OUT
JIM DAVIS

© 1978 PAWS, INC. All Rights Reserved.
SCRATCH
SCRATCH
SCRATCH
SCRATCH
SCRATCH
SCRATCH
8-18

JIM DAVIS
© 1978 PAWS, INC. All Rights Reserved.

THOCK!

NEW DANCE?
BAD AIM
8-19

GARFIELD®

WE CATS ARE THE SOURCE OF MANY MYTHS...

THE SAYING, "NERVOUS AS A CAT", IS AN OLD WIVE'S TALE.
8-20

BARK!

© 1978 PAWS, INC. All Rights Reserved.

NOT TO MENTION, "A CAT ALWAYS LANDS ON HIS FEET".
JIM DAVIS

HEH, HEH, HEH
SPLASH
SPLASH
SPLASH
© 1978 PAWS, INC. All Rights Reserved.

CATS JUST LOVE TO PLAY WITH WATER
JIM DAVIS

WHEW! I THOUGHT I'D NEVER FIND JON'S WATCH
8-21

DAB
DAB
DAB
DAB
© 1978 PAWS, INC. All Rights Reserved.
JIM DAVIS

SPLASH!
SPLASH!
SPLASH
SPLASH!
SPLASH!

MY CHICKEN SOUP!
THE DEVIL MADE ME DO IT
8-22

HEY, JON! WHAT DO YOU THINK OF MY NEW OUTFIT?

8-23

DOES GARFIELD ALWAYS SHED LIKE THAT?
ONLY ON WHITE DISCO SUITS
© 1978 PAWS, INC. All Rights Reserved.
JIM DAVIS

MUNCH
MUNCH
MUNCH
GARFIELD
ODIE
© 1978 PAWS, INC. All Rights Reserved.
8-24

PUNT
GARFIELD
ODIE

GOTTA KEEP MY STRENGTH UP
ELD
ODIE
JIM DAVIS

8-25

© 1978 PAWS, INC. All Rights Reserved.
JIM DAVIS

© 1978 PAWS, INC. All Rights Reserved.

SPLOOCH!
8-26

HELP YOURSELF TO THE LASAGNA, GARFIELD.
JIM DAVIS

GARFIELD®

YOU'RE GETTING A LITTLE CHUNKY THERE, PAL

I'M THINKING OF PUTTING YOU ON A DIET, GARFIELD.
© 1978 PAWS, INC. All Rights Reserved.

DIET!

I'M ALREADY FEELING WEAK!

FOOD! I NEED FOOD!

THE ROOM'S GROWING DIM!
8-27 ®

WHOP!

CLAP
CLAP
CLAP
CLAP
CLAP
CLAP
JIM DAVIS

GARFIELD, AS OF THIS MINUTE, I'M PUTTING YOU ON A DIET
8-28

GARFIELD?
© 1978 PAWS, INC. All Rights Reserved.

I THINK I SNAPPED HIS MIND
JIM DAVIS

COME ON, OLD BUDDY. GOING ON A DIET'S NOT ALL THAT BAD. WHY, A COUPLE OF POUNDS OFF THE MIDDLE AND YOU'LL BE FIT AND TRIM AGAIN
8-29
© 1978 PAWS, INC. All Rights Reserved.

THAT'S BETTER
JIM DAVIS

I DIDN'T HAVE THE HEART TO TELL HIM HE'S MADE THE WEIGHT WATCHER'S TEN MOST-WANTED LIST

SO I'M ON A DIET... BIG DEAL
© 1978 PAWS, INC. All Rights Reserved.
8-30

YOU KNOW WHAT A "DIET" IS, DON'T YOU?

IT'S "DIE" WITH A "T," THAT'S WHAT IT IS!
JIM DAVIS

A DIET. JON HAS ME ON A DIET
© 1978 PAWS, INC. All Rights Reserved.
8-31

POOMP!!

WHEN THE LASAGNA CONTENT IN MY BLOOD GETS LOW, I GET MEAN
JIM DAVIS

9-1
© 1978 PAWS, INC. All Rights Reserved.

WAX!

EVERYTHING TASTES GOOD WHEN YOU'RE ON A DIET
JIM DAVIS

LET'S SEE HOW WELL YOU'VE DONE ON YOUR DIET THIS WEEK, GARFIELD
© 1978 PAWS, INC. All Rights Reserved.

NOW WHERE'S THE BATHROOM SCALE?

I'M SITTING ON IT
JIM DAVIS
9-2

GARFIELD®

I HATE SUMMER. I GOTTA BEAT THIS HEAT SOMEHOW.

AHHH, JON'S FAN...

JON'S SUN-GLASSES

JON'S HAT

SOME ICE CUBES AND JON'S OLD KIDDY POOL
JIM DAVIS

MORNIN', JON. HERE'S YOUR MAIL
® 9-3
© 1978 PAWS, INC. All Rights Reserved.

LABOR DAY, SHMABOR DAY. WHAT A DUMB DAY.
© 1978 PAWS, INC. All Rights Reserved.
9-4
JIM DAVIS

TO HIRE SOME JERK, THEN SEND HIM AWAY...

TO CELEBRATE WORK BY PLAYING ALL DAY.

© 1978 PAWS, INC. All Rights Reserved.
9-5
JIM DAVIS

9-6

JIM DAVIS

HEE-HEE-HEE
© 1978 PAWS, INC. All Rights Reserved.
9-7

HA-HA-HA-HA-HA

JIM DAVIS

AND THAT'S ALL FOR MYSTERY THEATER. ...GOOD NIGHT.
© 1978 PAWS, INC. All Rights Reserved.

CLICK!

CLICK!
GARFIELD! CUT THAT OUT!
9-8
JIM DAVIS

WHAT'RE YOU DOING TONIGHT, LYMAN?
I'M GONNA CATCH THE NEW FLICK DOWN AT THE BIJOU.
© 1978 PAWS, INC. All Rights Reserved.

IT'S ABOUT THIS KID WHO PUTS A TACK IN HIS TEACHER'S CHAIR, AND SHE SITS ON IT.
9-9

NOT MUCH OF A PLOT.
I SUPPOSE NOT. BUT I STILL ENJOY THE MOVIES WHERE THE BOY GETS THE GIRL IN THE END.
JIM DAVIS

GARFIELD®

BRINNNG!

9-10

MORNIN', LYMAN
GOOD MORNING, JON.

READY TO GO?
BE RIGHT WITH YOU
© 1978 PAWS, INC. All Rights Reserved.

GARFIEEELD!!
ZZZZ

RISE 'N' SHINE, OLD BUDDY. TIME TO GO JOGGING!
JIM DAVIS

WHERE'S GARFIELD?
I THINK I'LL LET HIM SLEEP IN

9-11

© 1978 PAWS, INC. All Rights Reserved.

LEG CRAMPS
JIM DAVIS

HMMMMM
9-12

SMACK!

© 1978 PAWS, INC. All Rights Reserved.
JIM DAVIS

PURRRR
9-13

PURRR!
© 1978 PAWS, INC. All Rights Reserved.

HAVE SOME LASAGNA, GARFIELD...
PURRRR
JIM DAVIS

© 1978 PAWS, INC. All Rights Reserved.
CRINKLE
RUSTLE
CRINKLE

GARFIELD, GET OUT OF THE TRASH
JIM DAVIS
9-14

BUZZZZZ
DARN BUGS
© 1978 PAWS, INC. All Rights Reserved.
9-15

SWAT!
SPLAT!

THANKS. I NEEDED THAT
JIM DAVIS

CATS MAKE BETTER PETS
BUT YOU NEED A DOG FOR PROTECTION
JIM DAVIS

© 1978 PAWS, INC. All Rights Reserved.
9-16

I HATE TO SEE A GROWN MAN CRY

GARFIELD®

JIM DAVIS

© 1978 PAWS, INC. All Rights Reserved.

SLAM!

9-17

VETERINARY CLINIC
SOMEHOW, THEY ALWAYS KNOW.

© 1978 PAWS, INC. All Rights Reserved.
BAT
BAT
JIM DAVIS

FWIP FWIP FWIP FWIP

I HATE MONDAYS.
9/18

HEY, GARFIELD. MEET HONDO THE PUPPET.
© 1978 PAWS, INC. All Rights Reserved.

HI, GARFIELD. YOU'RE SURE FAT! HA-HA-HA!

JIM DAVIS
9/19

I HATE SUMMER
JIM DAVIS

THE UNBEARABLE HEAT, STICKY CAR SEATS, HAY FEVER SEASON AND SCORCHED LAWNS...

NOT TO MENTION CURDLED KITTY MUNCHIES
9-20
© 1978 PAWS, INC. All Rights Reserved.

JIM DAVIS
9-21
Z
© 1978 PAWS, INC. All Rights Reserved.

SNORT, UH-OH!

OH
OW
EEP
IPP
OOH
AAH
OOCH

© 1978 PAWS, INC. All Rights Reserved.
9-22

SUNBURNED TUMMY.
JIM DAVIS

OH BOY, AT LAST. COLLEGE FOOTBALL SEASON
© 1978 PAWS, INC. All Rights Reserved.

I WOULD HAVE PLAYED COLLEGE FOOTBALL HAD IT NOT BEEN FOR MY BELIEFS...
JIM DAVIS
9/23

I DON'T BELIEVE IN BLEEDING ON SATURDAY!
HOW WOULD YOU LIKE TO BE UNNECESSARILY ROUGHED?

GARFIELD®

I HATE DOGS

LOOK AT THAT POOR MUTT...

®
ALL BUGGY-EYED AND PANT-Y AND SLOBBERY. IT'S JUST DISGUSTING
PANT PANT PANT
JIM DAVIS

HEH, HEH. HEH

HERE, ODIE. HAVE A STEAK
9-24
© 1978 PAWS, INC. All Rights Reserved.
PAT PAT

PANT PANT PANT

© 1978 PAWS, INC. All Rights Reserved.
9-25
FWIP!

FLUFF
FLUFF

GARFIELD! TIME TO EAT!

JIM DAVIS
I HATE MONDAYS.

ALL DOGS SHOULD BE BANNED FROM OUR COUNTRY...
© 1978 PAWS, INC. All Rights Reserved.
JIM DAVIS

THEY ARE NOISY, SILLY, SLOPPY, RUDE...

AND THEY'RE RUSTING OUR NATION'S FIRE HYDRANTS.
9-26

TUM, DEE-DUM, DEE-DUM
9-27

PUNT!

IF IT WEREN'T FOR MY NATURALLY SWEET NATURE, I'D MAKE LIFE ROUGH FOR THAT DOG.
JIM DAVIS
© 1978 PAWS, INC. All Rights Reserved.

JIM DAVIS
BBBBB

BARK!

© 1978 PAWS, INC. All Rights Reserved.
I'D HATE TO SEE THAT SUCKER'S BITE!
9-28

GARFIELD
© 1978 PAWS, INC. All Rights Reserved.
JIM DAVIS

BARK!
SPLAT!

IF GOD HAD INTENDED FOR DOGS TO BARK, HE WOULD HAVE GIVEN THEM ROOTS AND LEAVES.
GARFIELD
9-29

BIFF!
© 1978 PAWS, INC. All Rights Reserved.
9-30

BOP!

GARFIELD, ONE. ODIE, ONE.
SMACK! POKE!
JIM DAVIS

GARFIELD®

AHEM... MEE, MEE, MEE

MEEEYOWRRRRR

BLINK
BLINK

SHADDUP, YOU STUPID CAT!

WING!

THOCK!

CHUNK!
JIM DAVIS

TOM SEAVER, EAT YOUR HEART OUT
10-1

SCRATCH
SCRATCH
SCRATCH
SCRATCH
SCRATCH
SCRATCH
SCRATCH
SCRATCH
SCRATCH
SCRATCH
SCRATCH
SCRATCH
SCRATCH
SCRATCH
SCRATCH

YAWN
10-5

THAT FLOOR SURE LOOKS COLD THIS MORNING
© 1978 PAWS, INC. All Rights Reserved.

BETTER NOT RISK IT
JIM DAVIS

I'M NOT GETTING OUT OF BED IF THE FLOOR IS COLD
10-6

IT'S FREEZING!
© 1978 PAWS, INC. All Rights Reserved.

GOOD
JIM DAVIS

ZZZZZ
10-7
© 1978 PAWS, INC. All Rights Reserved.

BARK!

NOW THAT I'M UP.. I MIGHT AS WELL HAVE BREAKFAST
JIM DAVIS

GARFIELD®

GOOD MORNING, GARFIELD

TODAY WE'RE GOING TO LEARN TO WALK ON A LEASH
JIM DAVIS
10-8

© 1978 PAWS, INC. All Rights Reserved.

KABONKA
BONKA
BONKA

ROWRR!

I TELL YOU, THELMA, THIS NEIGHBORHOOD IS GETTING WEIRDER BY THE MINUTE

BUZZZZZZZZZZZZZZZZZZZZ
ZZZZZZZZZZ
© 1978 PAWS, INC. All Rights Reserved.
10-9

ZZZZZZZZZ

SPLOOSH

I HATE MONDAYS
JIM DAVIS

© 1978 PAWS, INC. All Rights Reserved.
10-10

EVER THOUGHT OF WALKING **AROUND** THE FURNITURE?
JIM DAVIS

10-11
© 1978 PAWS, INC. All Rights Reserved.

OH WELL... I GUESS A CAT IS ENTITLED TO LET DOWN ON HIS DEFENSES ONCE IN HIS LIFE

JIM DAVIS

WATER
WATER
WATER
© 1978 PAWS, INC. All Rights Reserved.

PAT
PAT
PAT
10-12

WHAT'S THE USE?
JIM DAVIS

GARFIELD! I'M BACK FROM THE STORE
JIM DAVIS
© 1978 PAWS, INC. All Rights Reserved.

WE'RE HAVING A COOKOUT TONIGHT. I GOT STEAK AND CORN AND...

AND YOU JUST ATE THE BRIQUETTES
10-13

© 1978 PAWS, INC. All Rights Reserved.
10-14

CATS ARE NICE TO HAVE WHEN YOU'RE FEELING LONELY
JIM DAVIS

GARFIELD®

© 1978 PAWS, INC. All Rights Reserved.

BLINK!

I WIN AGAIN
JIM DAVIS
10-15

10-16

I THINK I'LL HAVE GARFIELD DECLAWED
© 1978 PAWS, INC. All Rights Reserved.
JIM DAVIS

GARFIELD, I'M GOING TO HAVE YOU DECLAWED
10-17

TAKE AN ARM! TAKE A LEG! BUT SPARE MY CLAWS!

YOU'RE GOING TO BE DECLAWED AND THAT'S THAT. NOW GET YOUR HEAD OUT OF THE OVEN!
JIM DAVIS
© 1978 PAWS, INC. All Rights Reserved.

I COULDN'T FACE LIFE AS A DECLAWED PERSON. SO I'LL JUST STICK MY HEAD IN THIS OVEN AND END IT ALL

10-18

© 1978 PAWS, INC. All Rights Reserved.
STUPID ELECTRIC STOVE
JIM DAVIS

JON'S GONNA HAVE ME DECLAWED
© 1978 PAWS, INC. All Rights Reserved.
10-19

WHAT A FRIGHTENING THOUGHT...

GOING THROUGH LIFE UNARMED
JIM DAVIS

I TOOK GARFIELD TO THE VET TO BE DECLAWED
© 1978 PAWS, INC. All Rights Reserved.
10-20

THEY'RE REMOVING HIS STITCHES NEXT THURSDAY

POOR GARFIELD
WHO'S TALKING ABOUT GARFIELD?
JIM DAVIS

I'M SORRY I TRIED TO HAVE YOU DECLAWED, GARFIELD

I LOVE YOU JUST THE WAY YOU ARE, CLAWS AND ALL

10-21
© 1978 PAWS, INC. All Rights Reserved.
SOMEDAY, SOMEHOW, WHEN YOU'RE LEAST EXPECTING IT, I'M GOING TO SHRED YOUR BEDROOM SUITE
JIM DAVIS

GARFIELD®

OHHH, GARFIEEELD!

AHA!
10-22

PUFF
PUFF

GOT'CHA!

© 1978 PAWS, INC. All Rights Reserved.

GARFIELD!
COME BACK HERE AND TAKE YOUR VITAMIN PILL!
JIM DAVIS

HELLO, WHAT'S THIS?

A TEDDY BEAR. A DUMB, STUPID, SILLY-LOOKING OLD TEDDY BEAR
© 1978 PAWS, INC. All Rights Reserved.

I THINK I'LL CALL HIM "POOKY"
JIM DAVIS
10-23

© 1978 PAWS, INC. All Rights Reserved.
10-24

I DIDN'T SEE THAT.
I DIDN'T SEE THAT.
I DIDN'T SEE THAT.
I DIDN'T SEE
JIM DAVIS

© 1978 PAWS, INC. All Rights Reserved.
10-25

GET AWAY FROM MY FOOD, BEAR!

I JUST YELLED AT A TEDDY BEAR
JIM DAVIS

NO, GARFIELD. I WILL NOT KISS YOUR TEDDY BEAR GOOD NIGHT
10-26

SMACK
© 1978 PAWS, INC. All Rights Reserved.
JIM DAVIS

AHHH...NOTHING LIKE A HOT BATH AFTER A CHILLY DAY
© 1978 PAWS, INC. All Rights Reserved.

GARFIELD!
WANNA WARM UP, POOKY?
JIM DAVIS
10-27

© 1978 PAWS, INC. All Rights Reserved.
OH BOY! MY BACHELOR MAGAZINE
JIM DAVIS

I WONDER WHO THE CENTERFOLD IS: ELKE? FARRAH?

ALMIRA, THE AMAZON?
10-28

GARFIELD®

IT'S THAT TIME OF YEAR AGAIN...

AT HALLOWEEN WE CATS BECOME BEWITCHED...

OUR EYES TURN BLOOD RED...
10-29

OUR FANGS GROW...

AND OUR HAIR STANDS UP.
© 1978 PAWS, INC. All Rights Reserved.
JIM DAVIS

NOT TO MENTION LONGER CLAWS

®

AAYIEEE!

THAT'S RIGHT, DOC. HE SCREAMED, TURNED WHITE, AND PASSED OUT.

AH, HERE COMES THE MAILMAN
10-30

DRAT!

© 1978 PAWS, INC. All Rights Reserved.
JIM DAVIS

BARK!
© 1978 PAWS, INC. All Rights Reserved.
JIM DAVIS

ODIE! CUT THAT OUT!

STICK WITH ME, KID. WE'LL GO PLACES
10-31

I HATE NOVEMBER
© 1978 PAWS, INC. All Rights Reserved.

LIFELESS TREES, BLEAK AFTERNOONS, RAW WINDS...

ICY SANDBOXES
11-1
JIM DAVIS

© 1978 PAWS, INC. All Rights Reserved.
KABOING!
KABOING!
KABOING!
GARFIELD

KABOING!
KABOING!
KABOING!
KABOING!
GARFIELD

FOOD'S FUN!
GARFIELD
11-2
JIM DAVIS

© 1978 PAWS, INC. All Rights Reserved.
SCREEEE!

FOUR PLY, STEEL-BELTED, RADIAL RETREAD TENNY PUMPS

ZOOOOOM!
11-3
JIM DAVIS

11-4

ZIP!

THAT HURT ME MORE THAN IT DID HIM
JIM DAVIS
© 1978 PAWS, INC. All Rights Reserved.

GARFIELD

GARFIELD!!

HMMMM
A LITTLE NIPPY OUTSIDE TODAY

BUT I **GOTTA** GET SOME EXERCISE
TAP TAP TAP
11-5

I CAN WAIT

MIGHT AS WELL GET IT OVER WITH
JIM DAVIS

AND THEN AGAIN...

MAKE UP YOUR MIND!

SOME PEOPLE HAVE ANXIETY ATTACKS. SOME PEOPLE HAVE GAS ATTACKS
JIM DAVIS

I HAVE NAP ATTACKS

© 1978 PAWS, INC. All Rights Reserved.
11-6
ZZZZZ

© 1978 PAWS, INC. All Rights Reserved.
NAP ATTACK!
JIM DAVIS

FUMP!

I'VE HEARD OF CATNAPS, BUT THIS IS RIDICULOUS
ZZZZ
11-7

NAP ATTACK!
© 1978 PAWS, INC. All Rights Reserved.

CRASH!

WHOEVER THOUGHT A NAP ATTACK COULD HURT?
11-8
JIM DAVIS

MY TUNA PÂTÉ COULD USE SOME SALT
GARFIELD
© 1978 PAWS, INC. All Rights Reserved.
11-9

OOPS! HERE COMES ANOTHER NAP ATTACK
GARFIELD

THERE YOU HAVE IT. GARFIELD'S PASSION FOR FOOD IS ONLY EXCEEDED BY HIS PASSION FOR SLEEP
ZZZZZZZZ
GARFIELD
JIM DAVIS

GEE, I'D LOVE TO STAY IN BED ALL DAY, BUT I GOTTA EAT SOMETIME
© 1978 PAWS, INC. All Rights Reserved.
11-10

BUZZ
SAW
SAW
SCRATCH
SCRATCH
CUT
CUT
BZZZ

GARFIELD
JIM DAVIS

OH-OH. I FEEL A NAP ATTACK COMING ON
© 1978 PAWS, INC. All Rights Reserved.
11-11

TURTLES HAVE GOT IT KNOCKED
JIM DAVIS

GARFIELD®

WHY DON'T YOU BOYS GO FIGHT OR SOMETHING?
© 1978 PAWS, INC. All Rights Reserved.

HI, JON!
HI, LYMAN
SLAM!

I'M STARVED! WHAT'S TO EAT?
NOTHING. I'M EATING THE LAST OF THE FOOD
11-12

JIM DAVIS

ZZZZZ
SNORT!
ZZZZ
© 1978 PAWS, INC. All Rights Reserved.

MMMPH!
11-13

ARRRRRRRGH!
SLEEPING PEOPLE ARE FUN
JIM DAVIS

I LOVE LASAGNA
SO DO I
11-14

GOBBLE! GOBBLE! GOBBLE! GOBBLE!
© 1978 PAWS, INC. All Rights Reserved.

I LOVE CATS. I WANTED A CAT... SO WHAT DO I DO? I GO TO THE PET STORE AND ASK FOR A CAT. WHAT DO THEY GIVE ME?...A LASAGNA WITH FUR AND FANGS
JIM DAVIS

CATS NEED A BALANCED DIET
© 1978 PAWS, INC. All Rights Reserved.

MEAT, EGGS, FRUIT, BREAD, VEGETABLES...

AND AN OCCASIONAL BOSTON FERN FOR DESSERT
11-15
JIM DAVIS

11-16
OH NO! JON GOT A ROCKING CHAIR!
© 1978 PAWS, INC. All Rights Reserved.
JIM DAVIS

AS LONG AS THERE IS ONE ROCKING CHAIR LEFT IN THIS WORLD, NO CAT'S TAIL IS SAFE

MY ROCKING CHAIR!
YOUR KINDLING

LET'S SEE...THE PIANO, BOOK SHELVES, BENCH, FLOOR...
© 1978 PAWS, INC. All Rights Reserved.

NOPE, I THINK I'LL GO WITH THE CHEST, CHAIR, HASSOCK, FLOOR

JIM DAVIS
11-17

HMMM...ONE CANISTER IS DOGGIE BISCUITS AND THE OTHER IS KITTY MUNCHIES, BUT I FORGET WHICH IS WHICH
11-18
© 1978 PAWS, INC. All Rights Reserved.

WHAM!

JIM DAVIS

GARFIELD®

MEYOWR!
BARK!

ROWR!
FFFT! ROWR!
BARK! BARK!

HOLD IT DOWN, YOU GUYS

MEYOWR
WOOF

ROWR!
FFFT! ROWR!
BARK! BARK!

ONE MORE SOUND OUT OF YOU TWO, AND YOU'RE IN BIG TROUBLE!
© 1978 PAWS, INC. All Rights Reserved.
11-19

RING!

HELLO?

BARK! ROWR!
JIM DAVIS

AHHH, SIX A.M.
© 1978 PAWS, INC. All Rights Reserved.
11-20

THIS IS MY FAVORITE TIME OF DAY

FOR SLEEP
JIM DAVIS

11-21
© 1978 PAWS, INC. All Rights Reserved.

GARFIELD!
HE SURE WAKES UP IN A BAD MOOD, DOESN'T HE?
JIM DAVIS

I LOVE SCRAMBLED EGGS
© 1978 PAWS, INC. All Rights Reserved.

ESPECIALLY ON CHILLY MORNINGS...

WHEN MY FEET GET COLD
11-22
JIM DAVIS

I'M BASICALLY YOUR NEAT CAT

CRASH!

I LIKE TO KEEP MY WINDOWSILL TIDY
11-23
© 1978 PAWS, INC. All Rights Reserved.
JIM DAVIS

WE CATS ARE LONERS
© 1978 PAWS, INC. All Rights Reserved.

WITH ONE POSSIBLE EXCEPTION...

WE CAN BE VERY SOCIAL WHEN IT COMES TO FOOD
11-24
JIM DAVIS

OKAY, GARFIELD, JUST ONE BITE OF LASAGNA AND THAT'S IT

© 1978 PAWS, INC. All Rights Reserved.

IT'S AMAZING HOW MUCH THAT CAT CAN STORE IN HIS CHEEKS
11-25
JIM DAVIS

GARFIELD®

AHA!

TO BE SURE YOU STAY AWAY FROM MY PIE, I'M GOING TO PUT THIS BELL AROUND YOUR NECK
DING-A-LING A-LING A-LING

I SHOULD HAVE THOUGHT OF THIS LONG AGO
DING-A-LING A-LING A-LING

HEH-HEH, GARFIELD IS IN THE BEDROOM NOW
DING-A-LING A-LING A-LING
© 1978 PAWS, INC. All Rights Reserved.
11-26

HE'S GOING THROUGH THE BATHROOM
DING-A-LING A-LING A-LING

NOW HE'S COMING DOWN THE HALL INTO THE LIVING ROOM
DING-A-LING A-LING
®

DING-A-LING A-LING A-LING

NO DING-A-LING'S GOING TO KEEP ME FROM MY PIE
JIM DAVIS

OH DOE!
SNIFF
11-27

I THIG I HAB A CODE
SNIFF
© 1978 PAWS, INC. All Rights Reserved.

LOOG..EBEN MY THOUGHTS ARE STUFFED UB
JIM DAVIS

SNIFF
HACK
COUGH
WHEEZE
© 1978 PAWS, INC. All Rights Reserved.
JIM DAVIS

11-28

SNIFF
HACK
COUGH
WHEEZE

HACK
SNIFF
WHEEZE
SNIFF
© 1978 PAWS, INC. All Rights Reserved.
11-29

GOBBLE!
GOBBLE!
GOBBLE!
GOBBLE!

OR IS IT: STARVE A COLD, FEED A FEVER?
JIM DAVIS

WAH-
CHOO!

WAH-
CHOO!

GARFIELD®

BRRR!

YAWN!
12-3

I KNOW YOU'RE IN THERE SOMEWHERE, GARFIELD!... OUT!!!

NEXT TIME I'LL LEAVE A WAKE-UP CALL AT THE DESK
JIM DAVIS
© 1978 PAWS, INC. All Rights Reserved.

DO YOU KNOW YOUR CAT'S SITTING ON MY MEAT LOAF ?
12-4

NO, BUT IF YOU HUM A COUPLE OF BARS I'LL FAKE IT
© 1978 PAWS, INC. All Rights Reserved.

THIS IS GOING TO BE A LONG WEEK
JIM DAVIS

SEE YOU LATER, GARFIELD. I'M GOING TO THE GROCERY STORE

© 1978 PAWS, INC. All Rights Reserved.
VERY WELL, YOU MAY COME ALONG
12-5
JIM DAVIS

NOW, BEHAVE YOURSELF IN THE GROCERY STORE, GARFIELD

JIM DAVIS

I THINK I JUST TURNED A BULL LOOSE IN A CHINA SHOP
© 1978 PAWS, INC. All Rights Reserved.
12-6

THAT'S THE LAST TIME I TAKE YOU TO THE GROCERY STORE, GARFIELD

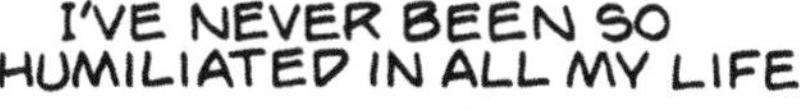
I'VE NEVER BEEN SO HUMILIATED IN ALL MY LIFE

12-7

SO I ATE THE PASTRY SECTION, BIG DEAL
JIM DAVIS
© 1978 PAWS, INC. All Rights Reserved.

ODIE
12-8

DARN
ODIE
© 1978 PAWS, INC. All Rights Reserved.

THAT WAS TOO EASY
ODIE
JIM DAVIS

WHEN ODIE COMES BY I'M GOING TO ROUND OFF THAT POINTY HEAD OF HIS
12-9

SLURP!
© 1978 PAWS, INC. All Rights Reserved.

HOW CAN YOU WIN AGAINST SOMEONE WHO DOESN'T EVEN KNOW THE RULES OF THE GAME ?
JIM DAVIS

GARFIELD®

© 1978 PAWS, INC. All Rights Reserved.

HERE, ODIE!
12-10
JIM DAVIS

ISN'T IT A LITTLE COLD TO TAKE ODIE FOR A WALK?
NONSENSE!

THINGS TO DO:
1. wash car
2. do laundry
12-11

© 1978 PAWS, INC. All Rights Reserved.

3. and brush Garfield
JIM DAVIS

I OWN A CAT
12-12
© 1978 PAWS, INC. All Rights Reserved.

AND WHEN YOU OWN A CAT, EATING A NORMAL MEAL TAKES ON AN ALL-NEW PERSPECTIVE

KNOWING THAT SOMEWHERE IN THERE IS A CAT HAIR WITH YOUR NAME ON IT
JIM DAVIS

I'M GOING TO BRUSH ALL YOUR LOOSE HAIR OUT, GARFIELD
12-13

© 1978 PAWS, INC. All Rights Reserved.

I SUSPECTED AS MUCH
JIM DAVIS

SWEEP
SWEEP
SWEEP
SWEEP
SWEEP
JIM DAVIS
12-14
© 1978 PAWS, INC. All Rights Reserved.

GARFIELD, WHAT AM I SUPPOSED TO DO WITH ALL THESE CAT HAIRS ?!
MAKE YOURSELF ANOTHER CAT

I HAVE THE DISTINCT FEELING THAT I WAS JUST ZINGED

12-15
GOOD NIGHT, GARFIELD
SMACK!
JIM DAVIS

POOEY!
© 1978 PAWS, INC. All Rights Reserved.

GROWING A BEARD?
I ATE A MILK DUD AND KISSED A CAT

Dear Garfield,
Help! I have cat hairs all over my home. What can I do to keep Fluffy from shedding?

SIMPLE
12-16
© 1978 PAWS, INC. All Rights Reserved.

GIVE THE LITTLE BEGGAR A GOOD COAT OF VARNISH
JIM DAVIS

GARFIELD®

SCRATCH
SCRATCH
SCRATCH
SCRATCH
SCRATCH

UH-OH
12-17

JUST LOOK WHAT YOU'VE DONE TO MY CHAIR!

YOU SHOULD BE MORE CONSIDERATE OF OTHER PEOPLE'S PROPERTY

NOW I KNOW IT'S NATURAL FOR CATS TO SHARPEN THEIR CLAWS

FISH GOTTA SWIM, BIRDS GOTTA FLY, AND CATS GOTTA CLAW. BUT DO IT OUTSIDE, OKAY?
JIM DAVIS

GARFIELD?

© 1978 PAWS, INC. All Rights Reserved.
GAR-FIELD

12-18
JIM DAVIS
ZZZZZZ

YAWN!

WHAT A HECK OF A WAY TO WAKE UP
© 1978 PAWS, INC. All Rights Reserved.

12-19

© 1978 PAWS, INC. All Rights Reserved.

JIM DAVIS

I KNOW CATS ARE FAST, BUT **THAT'S** RIDICULOUS

© 1978 PAWS, INC. All Rights Reserved.
JON! COME QUICK!
12-20

LOOK! GARFIELD IS ACTUALLY PLAYING WITH ODIE!
I KNOW. IT'S 'CAUSE I SPRAYED ODIE WITH SOMETHING

WITH WHAT?
ESSENCE OF LASAGNA
JIM DAVIS

YOU KNOW, MAYBE THERE'S MORE TO LIFE THAN JUST EATING AND SLEEPING... MAYBE I SHOULD BE MORE CONSIDERATE OF OTHER PEOPLE'S FEELINGS, NICER TO ODIE AND MORE GENEROUS

© 1978 PAWS, INC. All Rights Reserved.
NAH
JIM DAVIS
12-21

SCRATCHING POSTS, BALLS OF YARN AND RUBBER MOUSIES ARE OKAY
12-22
JIM DAVIS

BUT WHEN IT COMES TO **REALLY NEAT** PLAYTHINGS...
© 1978 PAWS, INC. All Rights Reserved.

GIVE ME A CHRISTMAS TREE!

WHAT WOULD YOU LIKE FOR CHRISTMAS, GARFIELD?
100 SLAVE DOGS
12-23

I'LL BET YOU'D LIKE A NICE, FLUFFY BALL OF YARN TO PLAY WITH

I THINK I'LL PUT A PIRANHA IN HIS CHRISTMAS STOCKING
JIM DAVIS
© 1978 PAWS, INC. All Rights Reserved.

GARFIELD®

HO-HO-HO

HO-HO-HO
© 1978 PAWS, INC. All Rights Reserved.

WHUMP!

LET'S SEE, GIFTS FOR JON, LYMAN AND ODIE

HMMM

OH YES, AND GARFIELD
JIM DAVIS
12-24

HOW COULD I EVER FORGET, GARFIELD...

ONLY KID IN THE WORLD TO ASK FOR 20 POUNDS OF LASAGNA

THIS IS MY VERY FIRST CHRISTMAS
12-25

I HOPE YOU HAVE A LOVED ONE TO SPEND TODAY WITH BECAUSE I DO
© 1978 PAWS, INC. All Rights Reserved.

IT'S YOU. MERRY CHRISTMAS
JIM DAVIS

OKAY, GARFIELD. GO FETCH!
12-26
JIM DAVIS

© 1978 PAWS, INC. All Rights Reserved.

TIME TO GET UP, GARFIELD
ZZZZ
12-27

GRRRRR

© 1978 PAWS, INC. All Rights Reserved.
NOW WHAT DO I DO?
ZZZZ
JIM DAVIS

© 1978 PAWS, INC. All Rights Reserved.
12-28

PUSH

I'M NOT KNOWN FOR MY COMPASSION
CLONK!
JIM DAVIS

I LOVE FRIDAYS
© 1978 PAWS, INC. All Rights Reserved.
12-29

THE END OF A LONG WORK WEEK, THE BEGINNING OF A WEEKEND FILLED WITH RELAXATION, TV SPORTS AND PARTIES

ALMOST MAKES ME WISH I HAD A JOB
JIM DAVIS

THIS YEAR I RESOLVE TO BE NICER TO DOGS
© 1978 PAWS, INC. All Rights Reserved.
12-30

MAYBE I'LL CUT DOWN ON LASAGNA INSTEAD
JIM DAVIS

GARFIELD®

IT'S TIME TO MAKE A NEW YEAR'S RESOLUTION, GARFIELD

I RESOLVE TO LOSE WEIGHT AND TO START EXERCISING THIS YEAR
JIM DAVIS
12-31

WHAT AM I SAYING ?!

I MUST BE GOING WAKA-WAKA!

I'M **NOT** GOING TO DIET!... I'M **NOT** GOING TO EXERCISE!

I'M FAT, AND I'M LAZY, AND I'M PROUD OF IT!

WHERE'S GARFIELD?
HE ATE THE BUFFET AND WENT TO BED

POW!
1-1

© 1979 PAWS, INC. All Rights Reserved.
JIM DAVIS

WHAT WOULD YOU LIKE FOR BREAKFAST, GARFIELD?
A CUP OF COFFEE, A DANISH AND THE NEWSPAPER
© 1979 PAWS, INC. All Rights Reserved.

HAVE A WARM BOWL OF MILK

YOU PEOPLE DON'T GIVE US CATS ANY CREDIT!
JIM DAVIS
1-2

DO YOU KNOW WHY I DON'T LIKE WARM MILK?
© 1979 PAWS, INC. All Rights Reserved.

TRY THIS... DRINK A BOWL OF WARM MILK

THEN, NEVER BRUSH YOUR TEETH AGAIN
JIM DAVIS
1-3

WHY IS IT ALL US CATS ARE STEREOTYPED?
© 1979 PAWS, INC. All Rights Reserved.

"ALL CATS LOVE MILK, HATE DOGS, LOVE MICE" ETC., ETC., ETC.

SOMETIMES I GET SO MAD I COULD JUST KICK MY GUCCI SCRATCHING POST
1-4
JIM DAVIS

JIM DAVIS
1-5
DO YOU KNOW WHY YOU NEED ME, GARFIELD?

© 1979 PAWS, INC. All Rights Reserved.
I CAN SUM IT UP IN TWO WORDS

QUALITY COMPANIONSHIP
BODY HEAT

WE CATS ARE VERY INDEPENDENT
1-6

© 1979 PAWS, INC. All Rights Reserved.
WE NEED NOBODY, NO TIME NO WHERE, NO WAY

JIM DAVIS
ISN'T THAT RIGHT, POOKY?

GARFIELD®

WHAT, HO?

OH, GOODY. A BLUEBERRY MUFFIN
© 1979 PAWS, INC. All Rights Reserved.

ZIPPPPP

SCRATCH
SCRATCH
SCRATCH

KICK!

CRA-SH!

IF YOU'LL PARDON THE EXPRESSION, THERE'S MORE THAN ONE WAY TO SKIN A CAT
1-7
JIM DAVIS

LOOK WHAT MY MOTHER MADE FOR YOU, GARFIELD
1-8

THERE, HOW'S THAT?
IT'S NICE AND WARM

DISGUSTING, DEMEANING, ITCHY AND AN ABOMINATION. BUT, NICE AND WARM
JIM DAVIS
© 1979 PAWS, INC. All Rights Reserved.

WOULD YOU JUST LOOK AT THIS? JON'S MAKING ME WEAR A KITTY SWEATER
JIM DAVIS
© 1979 PAWS, INC. All Rights Reserved.

PEOPLE DRESS THEIR PETS UP BECAUSE IT MAKES THEM LOOK LIKE LITTLE PEOPLE. WELL, I'M **NOT** A LITTLE PERSON, I'M A **CAT**
1-9

FOR INSTANCE, I LIKE A PINCH OF CATNIP IN MY MORNING CUP OF COFFEE

HERE HE COMES. SAY SOMETHING NICE
© 1979 PAWS, INC. All Rights Reserved.
1-10

LOOKIN' GOOD, GARFIELD
SHARP SWEATER, OL' BUDDY

SAD
LOOKS LIKE A MEATBALL IN TRACTION
JIM DAVIS

I WAS FEELING PRETTY PUNK ABOUT HAVING TO WEAR THIS SWEATER...
© 1979 PAWS, INC. All Rights Reserved.

UNTIL I SAW ODIE'S NEW OUTFIT
1-11

JIM DAVIS

UH-OH, IT'S STARTING TO RAIN
© 1979 PAWS, INC. All Rights Reserved.
JIM DAVIS

I'D BETTER LET GARFIELD IN BEFORE HE GETS HIS NEW SWEATER WET
1-12

TOO LATE

SNICKER SNICKER
© 1979 PAWS, INC. All Rights Reserved.

HARF! HARF! HARF!

JIM DAVIS
1-13

GARFIELD®

WHEN YOU OWN A CAT, ITS HAIRS GET EVERYWHERE

EVERY TIME I EAT, I FIND A CAT HAIR IN MY FOOD. LET ME SHOW YOU
JIM DAVIS

I KNOW IT'S HERE SOMEWHERE
1-14

© 1979 PAWS, INC. All Rights Reserved.

I CAN'T EAT 'TIL I FIND THAT HAIR!

SILLY ME. I FORGOT TO PUT IT IN THERE

1-15
JIM DAVIS
© 1979 PAWS, INC. All Rights Reserved.

GARFIELD, YOU SHOULDN'T CHASE THE MAILMAN LIKE THAT

NOW WHAT WOULD YOU DO WITH HIM IF YOU ACTUALLY CAUGHT HIM?
I'D EAT HIM

GARFIELD, YOU KNOW CATS CAN'T DRINK...
1-16
© 1979 PAWS, INC. All Rights Reserved.

...COFFEE
SLURP!

FILL'ER UP
WELL, I'LL BE DIPPED
JIM DAVIS

© 1979 PAWS, INC. All Rights Reserved.
JIM DAVIS

IT'S AMAZING HOW WE'VE GROWN TO UNDERSTAND ONE ANOTHER
1-17

LOOK, GARFIELD. A MOUSE!
1-18

EEEK!

© 1979 PAWS, INC. All Rights Reserved.
JIM DAVIS

BACHELORHOOD IS OKAY, I GUESS
1-19
JIM DAVIS

BUT YOU JUST CAN'T BEAT...
© 1979 PAWS, INC. All Rights Reserved.

SOMEONE WAITING FOR YOU WHEN YOU GET HOME

BARK! BARK!
© 1979 PAWS, INC. All Rights Reserved.
1-20

ROWR! YAP! FFFT!
JIM DAVIS

AND THEY SAY PETS ARE THERAPEUTIC

GARFIELD®

SCRATCH
SCRATCH
SCRATCH
SCRATCH

UH-OH.
FLEAS!

ALCOHOL SHOULD DO THE TRICK

MUCH BETTER
© 1979 PAWS, INC. All Rights Reserved.

PUFF
PUFF

FOOMP

THERE'S SOMETHING TO BE SAID FOR FLEA COLLARS
JIM DAVIS
1-21

GARFIELD, YOU SLEEP TOO MUCH, YOU EAT TOO MUCH, AND YOU WATCH TOO MUCH TELEVISION
1-22

WHAT DOES JON EXPECT OF ME, ANYWAY?

I'M ONLY HUMAN
JIM DAVIS
© 1979 PAWS, INC. All Rights Reserved.

© 1980 United Feature Syndicate, Inc.
JIM DAVIS

A Talk with Jim Davis: Most Asked Questions

How far in advance do you do the strip?

"Eight to ten weeks—no less, no more. I operate on what Al Capp termed 'the ragged edge of disaster.' "

When did GARFIELD first appear in newspapers?

"June 19, 1978."

Where do you get your ideas for the strip?

"I glean a lot of good ideas from fan mail. Cat owners are very proud of their cats and supply a generous amount of cat stories."

What GARFIELD products are on the market and in production?

"Books, calendars, T-shirts, coffee mugs, posters, tote bags, greeting cards, puzzles...in another few months GARFIELD will be on everything but pantyhose and TVs."

Why a cat?

"Aside from the obvious reasons, that I know and love cats, I noticed there were a lot of comic-strip dogs who were commanding their share of the comic pages but precious few cats. It seemed like a good idea."

Where did you get the name GARFIELD?

"My grandfather's name was James A. Garfield Davis. The name GARFIELD to me sounds like a fat cat...or a St. Bernard...or a neat line of thermal underwear."

What did you do for a living before GARFIELD?

"I was assistant on the comic strip TUMBLEWEEDS and a free-lance commercial artist."

What's your sign?

"Leo, of course, the sign of the cat."

Have you ever been convicted of a felony?

"Next question, please."

Are you subject to fainting spells, seizures, and palpitations?

"Only when I work."

Have you ever spent time in a mental institution?

"Yes, I visit my comics editor there."

Do you advocate the overthrow of our government by violent means?

"No, but I have given consideration to vandalizing my local license branch."

Are you hard of hearing?

"Huh?"

Do you wish to donate an organ?

"Heck no, but I have a piano I can let go cheap."

Garfield gains weight

BY: JIM DAVIS

JIM DAVIS
© 1979 PAWS, INC. All Rights Reserved.

TELEVISION CAN BE HABIT FORMING
JIM DAVIS
© 1979 PAWS, INC. All Rights Reserved.

I'VE BEEN WATCHING IT ALL DAY
1-23

WOULD YOU LIKE ME TO TURN THE TV ON, GARFIELD?
THAT WOULD BE NICE

WE'VE GOTTA STOP WATCHING THE ALL-NIGHT MOVIES ON TELEVISION, GARFIELD
1-24

BUT, OF COURSE, LAST NIGHT WAS AN EXCEPTION
© 1979 PAWS, INC. All Rights Reserved.

WHO COULD POSSIBLY TURN OFF THE ETHEL BARRYMORE FILM FESTIVAL?
JIM DAVIS

BANG!
BANG!
EEEK!
1-25

SMACK!
© 1979 PAWS, INC. All Rights Reserved.

OKAY, OKAY. I'LL CHANGE THE CHANNEL
I DON'T LIKE VIOLENCE
JIM DAVIS

I HATE TELEVISION
© 1979 PAWS, INC. All Rights Reserved.
1-26

THERE ARE TOO MANY COMMERCIALS, RERUNS AND GAME SHOWS
JIM DAVIS

THE EIGHT HOURS I WATCHED YESTERDAY WAS TERRIBLE

TELEVISION IS ONLY SO MUCH MINDLESS DRIVEL...
© 1979 PAWS, INC. All Rights Reserved.
1-27

GLOSSY ADVENTURES, SEX AND VIOLENCE

AIN'T IT GREAT?
JIM DAVIS

GARFIELD®

YAWN!

SMACK
SMACK
SMACK

OH MY

JUST LOOK AT THAT GORGEOUS SUNRISE!

MOTHER NATURE CERTAINLY USES EVERY COLOR ON HER VAST PALETTE TO PAINT A DAWN. TRULY BLESSED ARE WE, THE EARLY RISERS

HAVE YOU EVER SEEN A MORE BEAUTIFUL SUNSET, GARFIELD?

HMMM... I MUST HAVE OVERSLEPT
© 1979 PAWS, INC. All Rights Reserved.
JIM DAVIS
1-28

GARFIELD, YOU ARE DISGUSTINGLY, SLOVENLY, SLOPPY FAT
1-29

POOR JON

HE OBVIOUSLY HAS DISGUSTINGLY, SLOVENLY, SLOPPY FAT CONFUSED WITH "BIG-BONED"
JIM DAVIS
© 1979 PAWS, INC. All Rights Reserved.

BRENDA, MEET GARFIELD
HI, GARFIELD
© 1979 PAWS, INC. All Rights Reserved.

IS GARFIELD A PIG?
HE'S A CAT
1-30

OH, THAT **REALLY** HURTS
JIM DAVIS

1-31
AHHH

CRASH!

FACE IT, GARFIELD. WINDOWSILLS JUST AREN'T BUILT FOR US QUEEN-SIZED FELINES
© 1979 PAWS, INC. All Rights Reserved.
JIM DAVIS

IF YOU TAKE ONE BITE OF MY PIE, GARFIELD, I'LL SMACK YOUR FAT LITTLE PAWS
2-1
© 1979 PAWS, INC. All Rights Reserved.

IF I CAN'T HAVE IT, NEITHER CAN HE
JIM DAVIS

I'LL BET YOU CAN'T WAIT TO SEE WHAT KIND OF CAT FOOD YOU'RE HAVING FOR DINNER
I'LL BET I CAN
© 1979 PAWS, INC. All Rights Reserved.

HERE IT COMES...
YOU CAN CUT THE TENSION WITH A KNIFE
2-2

LIVER!
OH, HOORAY, HOP ABOUT, CLAP PAWS, SQUEAL WITH GLEE
LIVER
JIM DAVIS

NOW I WOULDN'T SAY YOU'RE FAT, GARFIELD...
2-3

BUT WHEN YOU SIT AROUND THE SOFA, YOU **SIT AROUND** THE SOFA

HEADS, HE LIVES. TAILS, HE DIES
KICK!
JIM DAVIS
© 1979 PAWS, INC. All Rights Reserved.

GARFIELD®

2-4

© 1979 PAWS, INC. All Rights Reserved.

LET'S SEE... IODINE, BAND-AIDS, GAUZE, BULLWHIP, SMALL STRAIT-JACKET, HELMET, PAN, SHAMPOO, GLOVES, RINSE, CONDITIONER, BLOW DRYER, BRASS KNUCKLES, TOWEL, ROPE, ELBOW PADS...
JIM DAVIS

GARFIELD'S BATH DAY?
GARFIELD'S BATH DAY

I THINK I'LL DO SOME JOGGING
© 1979 PAWS, INC. All Rights Reserved.
2-5

OKAY... **GO, FEET!**

HMMM, RECKON THE LITTLE SUCKERS JUST WEREN'T IN THE MOOD
JIM DAVIS

GARFIELD, I'D APPRECIATE IT IF YOU WOULDN'T READ OVER MY SHOULDER

2-6

JIM DAVIS
READ OVER MY SHOULDER?
© 1979 PAWS, INC. All Rights Reserved.

STAY AWAY FROM MY CHICKEN LEG, GARFIELD
AW, STUFF IT IN YOUR EAR
MROW FFT!
2-7

WHAT WAS THAT?!
© 1979 PAWS, INC. All Rights Reserved.

OH
JIM DAVIS

GEE... I WONDER WHICH SHIRT GOES BETTER WITH MY SLACKS
JIM DAVIS
2-8

LYMAN, COULD YOU GIVE ME YOUR OPINION ON SOMETHING?
SURE

WHAT CAN I DO FOR YOU?
FORGET IT
BEAU BRUMMELL LIVES
© 1979 PAWS, INC. All Rights Reserved.

2-9

HE'S TRYING TO TELL ME TO TURN THE HEAT UP
JIM DAVIS
© 1979 PAWS, INC. All Rights Reserved.

GUESS WHAT, GARFIELD? SOMEWHERE ON ME IS A KITTY MUNCHIE FOR YOU
JIM DAVIS

2-10
© 1979 PAWS, INC. All Rights Reserved.

MAYBE THAT WASN'T SUCH A GOOD IDEA
MUNCH MUNCH MUNCH

GARFIELD®

NAB!

I'M GOING TO GIVE YOU A BATH, GARFIELD
YOU AND WHAT ARMY?

2-11

© 1979 PAWS, INC. All Rights Reserved.

OKAY... I GIVE UP. YOU CAN GO
JIM DAVIS

SPLOOSH

I HATE COLD FLOORS IN THE MORNING
JIM DAVIS
2-12

NOBODY LIKES COLD FLOORS
© 1979 PAWS, INC. All Rights Reserved.

BUT WE CATS HAVE TO PUT TWICE AS MANY FEET ON THEM

PETS ARE GREAT TO HAVE ON COLD NIGHTS
© 1979 PAWS, INC. All Rights Reserved.
2-13

AS LONG AS YOU DON'T MIND...

THE CROWDED CONDITIONS
JIM DAVIS

BARK! YIP!
ROWR! FFFT!
JIM DAVIS

GARFIELD! ODIE! WHY DON'T YOU BOYS GO OUTSIDE TO FIGHT
2-14
© 1979 PAWS, INC. All Rights Reserved.

WHILE I LIE HERE AND QUIETLY BLEED TO DEATH

© 1979 PAWS, INC. All Rights Reserved.

GARFIELD! GET OFF THE PIANO!
2-15

TALK ABOUT STIFLING ONE'S CREATIVE TALENTS
JIM DAVIS

THERE'S ONE NICE THING ABOUT BEING A CAT AT THE DINNER TABLE
2-16

© 1979 PAWS, INC. All Rights Reserved.

EVERYTHING YOU TOUCH IS YOURS
JIM DAVIS

WHAT'S A SIX-LETTER WORD FOR "PAIN," GARFIELD?
JIM DAVIS
2-17

ARRRGH!!!
KROCK!

© 1979 PAWS, INC. All Rights Reserved.
IS THAT WITH THREE OR FOUR R'S?

GARFIELD®

© 1979 PAWS, INC. All Rights Reserved.
SCRUB
SCRUB
SCRUB
SCRUB

2-18
JIM DAVIS

CLICK!

GARFIELD! STOP!

IT'S BELOW FREEZING OUT THERE

YOU SAY YOU WANT ME TO EAT THIS HAMBURGER, POOKY?
© 1979 PAWS, INC. All Rights Reserved.

AND THIS CHICKEN? AND THIS LASAGNA?

YOU GOTTA GO A LONG WAY TO FIND A TEDDY BEAR AS GOOD AS OLD POOKY HERE
2-19
JIM DAVIS

SMACK!
JIM DAVIS

HEY YOU! COME BACK HERE AND FIGHT LIKE A TEDDY BEAR!

WHAT AM I SAYING?
2-20
© 1979 PAWS, INC. All Rights Reserved.

BE HONEST, POOKY. DO YOU THINK I'M GETTING A LITTLE PUDGY AROUND THE MIDDLE?
© 1979 PAWS, INC. All Rights Reserved.

2-21

NOT A LOT OF PERSONALITY, BUT HE CERTAINLY KNOWS WHEN TO KEEP HIS MOUTH SHUT
JIM DAVIS

2-22

A DANCING BEAR?
NEXT TIME, I GET TO LEAD
© 1979 PAWS, INC. All Rights Reserved.
JIM DAVIS

LET'S GO FOR A WALK, LITTLE FELLA
2-23

SMACK!
© 1979 PAWS, INC. All Rights Reserved.

WELL, I'LL BE. POOKY DOESN'T LIKE DOGS EITHER
JIM DAVIS

OKAY, WHO KNOCKED MY FERN OFF THE WINDOWSILL?!
© 1979 PAWS, INC. All Rights Reserved.

2-24

HIS LYING TO ME ISN'T HALF SO UPSETTING AS THE CREDIT HE'S GIVING MY INTELLIGENCE
JIM DAVIS

GARFIELD®

KABOING
KABOING
KABOING
© 1979 PAWS, INC. All Rights Reserved.

PURRR

GARFIELD

BAT
BAT

ROWR!
FFFT!

SCRATCH!
SCRATCH!
SCRATCH!
2·25

THAT SHOULD
HOLD YOU CAT FANS
FOR A WHILE
JIM DAVIS

STAND ASIDE, CAT. I KNOW KARATE!

2-26

AND I KNOW FAST AND FURIOUS
JIM DAVIS
© 1979 PAWS, INC. All Rights Reserved.

© 1979 PAWS, INC. All Rights Reserved.

SOME DAYS I'M JUST NOT IN THE MOOD TO BE ADORED
JIM DAVIS
2-27

WOULD PUDDY TAT WIKE A BOWL OF MILK?
© 1979 PAWS, INC. All Rights Reserved.

WOULD FUNNY WOOKING MAN WIKE A MILK BATH?

NEVER BE CONDESCENDING TO A CAT
JIM DAVIS
2-28

3-1

GARFIELD! DID YOU EAT MY CHICKEN?
© 1979 PAWS, INC. All Rights Reserved.

NO, OF COURSE NOT. IF YOU HAD, THERE WOULD BE SOME BONES LEFT
JIM DAVIS

BE CAREFUL AROUND THIS CLOCK, GARFIELD. IT'S AN OLD FAMILY HEIRLOOM

CRASH!
© 1979 PAWS, INC. All Rights Reserved.

ONE SMALL PUSH FOR CAT, ONE GIANT LEAP FOR GOOD TASTE
JIM DAVIS
3-2

WHERE WERE YOU, GARFIELD? I CALLED YOU AN HOUR AGO FOR DINNER
UH-OH
GARFIELD
JIM DAVIS
© 1979 PAWS, INC. All Rights Reserved.

GARFIELD
KLUNK!

YOU'VE GOT TO GET TO CAT FOOD BEFORE IT SETS UP
GARFIE
3-3

GARFIELD®

TIE
TIE

TIE
TIE
TIE

YANK
YANK

LEAP!
JIM DAVIS

SPROING!

BOOGA! BOOGA!
3-4
© 1979 PAWS, INC. All Rights Reserved.

KLONK!

THAT WAS A LOT OF TROUBLE BUT IT WAS WORTH IT

ZZZZ
YAWN
© 1979 PAWS, INC. All Rights Reserved.
3-5

ZZZZZ
JIM DAVIS

WHAT A HECK OF A WAY TO START THE WEEK

THE DARN TOASTER ISN'T WORKING AGAIN. I GUESS I'LL HAVE TO FIX IT
© 1979 PAWS, INC. All Rights Reserved. 3-6

WHAM!
WHAM!
WHAM!
WHAM!
WHAM!

FIRST, YOU HAVE TO GET ITS ATTENTION
JIM DAVIS

BREAKFAST IS ON, GARFIELD
© 1979 PAWS, INC. All Rights Reserved.
JIM DAVIS

CARRY ME

SOMETIMES I THINK I CATER TO GARFIELD TOO MUCH
GARFIELD
3-7

© 1979 PAWS, INC. All Rights Reserved.
3-8

THAT'S CALLED DISCO DANCING, GARFIELD
THANK HEAVENS

FOR A MINUTE THERE I THOUGHT HE HAD A LIVE CARP IN HIS JOCKEY SHORTS
JIM DAVIS

GARFIELD, THAT STEELY-EYED COWCAT, ROAMS INTO TOWN
© 1979 PAWS, INC. All Rights Reserved.
3-9

HE MOUNTS HIS FAITHFUL STEED, ODIE

ALL I NEED NOW IS A SUNSET
JIM DAVIS

© 1979 PAWS, INC. All Rights Reserved.
3-10

JUST WHEN YOU THINK YOU'VE SEEN YOUR CAT DO IT ALL...
JIM DAVIS

GARFIELD®

BUZZZZZZZZZZZZZZZZZ

SPLOOSH

SPLUTTER
SPLUTTER

FLOP!
3-11

PTOOEY!
PTOOEY!
PTOOEY!

WIPE
WIPE
© 1979 PAWS, INC. All Rights Reserved.

CRASH

IF I ACT CASUAL, MAYBE HE WON'T NOTICE
JIM DAVIS

© 1979 PAWS, INC. All Rights Reserved.
3-12

SWISH!

THE MOUTH IS QUICKER THAN THE HAND
JIM DAVIS

© 1979 PAWS, INC. All Rights Reserved.

KNOCK! KNOCK! KNOCK!

NOBODY HOME
3-13
JIM DAVIS

© 1979 PAWS, INC. All Rights Reserved.

I SUPPOSE I SHOULD LEARN TO LIKE ODIE

BUT I JUST CAN'T RESPECT ANYONE WHO TURNS AROUND THREE TIMES TO LIE DOWN
JIM DAVIS
3-14

© 1979 PAWS, INC. All Rights Reserved.
3-15

HMMM

JUST AS I SUSPECTED. THERE'S A TINY SIGN IN THERE SAYING, "SPACE FOR RENT"
JIM DAVIS

BARK! BARK! BARK!

THAT'S GOOD ENOUGH
SCREEE
POOMP!

THANKS FOR THE EXERCISE
PUNT!
© 1979 PAWS, INC. All Rights Reserved.
3-16
JIM DAVIS

© 1979 PAWS, INC. All Rights Reserved.

PAT PAT PAT PAT

YOU DIDN'T SEE THAT
3-17
JIM DAVIS

GARFIELD®

HMMM, JON'S DRAWING BOARD. HMMM, SOME PAPER. HMMM, SOME INK

I THINK THIS WORLD WOULD BE A NICER PLACE IN WHICH TO LIVE:
IF COUNTRIES COULD SETTLE THEIR DIFFERENCES WITHOUT HURTING ANYBODY.
IF EVERYONE SMILED AT EVEN PEOPLE THEY DIDN'T KNOW

IF NOBODY HAD TO STEAL.
IF PEOPLE LAUGHED MORE.
IF EVERYONE FED THEIR CATS ALL THE LASAGNA THEY COULD EAT.
IF WE ALL TOOK MORE PRIDE IN OUR HOMES AND OUR NEIGHBORHOODS
© 1979 PAWS, INC. All Rights Reserved.
3-18

IF WE RESPECTED OUR SENIOR CITIZENS MORE.
IF THERE WERE NO VIOLENCE IN MOVIES AND TELEVISION.
IF EVERYONE COULD READ AND WRITE.
IF FAMILIES TALKED MORE

IF FRIENDS HUGGED MORE.
IF EVERYONE STOPPED AT LEAST ONCE A WEEK TO STROKE A CAT.
AFTER ALL, WE'RE ALL IN THIS TOGETHER

HEY, GARFIELD

WHAT'S THIS?
OH, JUST SOME PAW PRINTS
JIM DAVIS

I'M GOING TO TEACH YOU TO DO SOME TRICKS THIS WEEK, GARFIELD
OVER MY DEAD BODY
GARFIELD
3-19
© 1979 PAWS, INC. All Rights Reserved.

SING FOR ME, GARFIELD
MROWR!
GARFIELD

VERY GOOD!
THERE WAS A BONE IN MY TUNA PÂTÉ
GARFIELD
JIM DAVIS

GARFIELD, GO FETCH MY PIPE, PAPER AND SLIPPERS
YES, SIR. RIGHT AWAY, SIR...
JIM DAVIS
© 1979 PAWS, INC. All Rights Reserved.

WHERE **IS** HE?

GARFIELD!
OKAY, OKAY. AS SOON AS I'M DONE WITH THE FINANCIAL SECTION
3-20

ROLL OVER, GARFIELD
YOU GOTTA BE KIDDING
© 1979 PAWS, INC. All Rights Reserved.

IF YOU ROLL OVER, I'LL GIVE YOU A DOUBLE HELPING OF LASAGNA

WHIRRRRRR!
JIM DAVIS
3-21

SPEAK, GARFIELD, SPEAK
© 1979 PAWS, INC. All Rights Reserved.
3-22

WHY, OF COURSE, JON. IS THERE ANY PARTICULAR TOPIC ON WHICH YOU'D LIKE TO CONVERSE?

B-B-B-B-B
JIM DAVIS

SIT UP AND BEG FOR THE KITTY MUNCHY, GARFIELD
3-23

TELL YOU WHAT. YOU GIVE ME THE MUNCHY AND I'LL LET YOU KEEP YOUR FACE

I KNEW WE COULD ARRIVE AT A MUTUALLY ACCEPTABLE COMPROMISE
JIM DAVIS
© 1979 PAWS, INC. All Rights Reserved.

DANCE FOR ME, GARFIELD
NOT A CHANCE
JIM DAVIS
© 1979 PAWS, INC. All Rights Reserved.

IF YOU WON'T, I'M SURE ODIE WOULD BE HAPPY TO

YOU HAVE TO KNOW WHAT MOTIVATES A CAT
THIS IS DEMEANING
TAPPITY TAPPITY
3-24

GARFIELD®

3-25
© 1979 PAWS, INC. All Rights Reserved.

SIGH

HO HUM
GARFIELD

EVER HAD ONE OF THOSE DAYS WHEN YOU FEEL LIKE YOU'VE SLEPT AND EATEN IT ALL?
JIM DAVIS

AH, IT'S EARLY MORNING FOR THE CAPED AVENGER
RING!
© 1979 PAWS, INC. All Rights Reserved.

THE CAPED AVENGER WHO SEARCHES OUT EVIL WHEREVER IT MAY LURK

THE LATE-MORNING EVIL, THAT IS
3-26
JIM DAVIS

THE CAPED AVENGER SEES FOOD!
© 1979 PAWS, INC. All Rights Reserved.
3-27

IN ORDER TO FIGHT EVIL, THE CAPED AVENGER NEEDS FOOD FOR STRENGTH

LOTS AND **LOTS** OF STRENGTH!
JIM DAVIS

AHA! THE CAPED AVENGER SEES INJUSTICE
BONK!

© 1979 PAWS, INC. All Rights Reserved.

BEAT IT, BRUTE
BOOT!
3-28
JIM DAVIS

THE CAPED AVENGER SEES A LARGE EVIL PERSON HE MUST DESTROY IN THE NAME OF GOOD, BECAUSE THE CAPED AVENGER ISN'T A CHICKEN

JIM DAVIS

© 1979 PAWS, INC. All Rights Reserved.
THE CAPED AVENGER ISN'T STUPID, EITHER
3-29

THE CAPED AVENGER WILL NOW FLY DOWN AND DESTROY THE EVIL MAILMAN
JIM DAVIS

SPLAT!

I THINK THE CAPED AVENGER IS STARTING TO BELIEVE HIS OWN PRESS RELEASES
© 1979 PAWS, INC. All Rights Reserved.
3-30

THE CAPED AVENGER WILL NOW STEP OUTSIDE TO FIGHT EVIL
3-31

THE CAPED AVENGER WILL NOW STEP INSIDE AND ANNOUNCE HIS RETIREMENT
JIM DAVIS
© 1979 PAWS, INC. All Rights Reserved.

GARFIELD®

I'M SO BORED

HMMMM

JIM DAVIS
PTUI
TWING!
YIP!
SPLOOSH!

BONK!

KICK!

MUCH BETTER
4-1
© 1979 PAWS, INC. All Rights Reserved.

DID YOU KNOW MOST CATS SHED THEIR WINTER COATS IN WARM WEATHER, GARFIELD?
4-2
© 1979 PAWS, INC. All Rights Reserved.

FUMP!

HMMM MUS' BE SPRING
JIM DAVIS

SPRING IS HERE

THE WARM SPRING SUN IS COAXING TREES TO BUD AND FLOWERS TO BLOOM. FLEDGLING SONGBIRDS ARE TESTING THEIR LILTING VOICES. SOFT SPRING ZEPHYRS ARE WAFTING THE SWEET SCENT OF LILACS. SPRING IS HERE

© 1979 PAWS, INC. All Rights Reserved.
BIG, FAT HAIRY DEAL
4-3
JIM DAVIS

THERE'S NOTHING LIKE A LITTLE SPRING WEATHER TO MAKE ONE FEEL LAZY
4-4
JIM DAVIS
© 1979 PAWS, INC. All Rights Reserved.

I'D BETTER BE CAREFUL

IF I WERE ANY LAZIER, I COULD SLIP INTO A COMA

I LIKE SPRING

THE GRASS IS BACK FROM ITS DORMANCY. THE FLOWERS ARE BACK FROM A LONG WINTER'S REST
© 1979 PAWS, INC. All Rights Reserved.
4-5

AND THE BIRDS ARE BACK FROM MIAMI
JIM DAVIS

I JUST LOVE TO LIE OUT IN THIS WARM SPRING SUN
4-6
JIM DAVIS

UH-OH

I THINK I JUST MELTED
© 1979 PAWS, INC. All Rights Reserved.

AH, SPRING. IN THE SPRING A YOUNG MAN'S FANCY TURNS LIGHTLY TO THOUGHTS OF LOVE
4-7

© 1979 PAWS, INC. All Rights Reserved.

AND THE STREET DEPARTMENT PUTS A FRESH COAT OF RUST-RESISTANT PAINT ON THE FIRE HYDRANTS
JIM DAVIS

GARFIELD®

CLICK

I'M GOING TO STARE AT THIS TOASTER UNTIL THE TOAST POPS UP

A WATCHED POT NEVER BOILS, GARFIELD
HUH?
POP
© 1979 PAWS, INC. All Rights Reserved.

SEE?
DRAT... DRAT, DRAT, DRAT, DRAT
JIM DAVIS
4-8

4-9
MOVE IT, GARFIELD. I'M GOING TO WATCH TELEVISION

© 1979 PAWS, INC. All Rights Reserved.

JIM DAVIS

BOY, AM I IN A BAD MOOD
GOOD MORNING, GARFIELD
4-10

POKE!
© 1979 PAWS, INC. All Rights Reserved.

IF THERE'S ANYTHING A DEPRESSED PERSON HATES, IT'S A CHEERFUL PERSON
JIM DAVIS

GARFIELD'S SURE BEEN IN A NASTY MOOD LATELY
WE'LL SEE ABOUT THAT. DO YOU KNOW HOW TO TREAT A MAD CAT?

4-11

WITH GREAT, GREAT RESPECT
JIM DAVIS
© 1979 PAWS, INC. All Rights Reserved.

4-12

ROWR!
FFFT!

I THINK I HURT MYSELF
© 1979 PAWS, INC. All Rights Reserved.
JIM DAVIS

I KNOW YOU'VE BEEN IN A NASTY MOOD THIS WEEK, GARFIELD. MANY OF US OCCASIONALLY FEEL ANGRY FOR NO REASON AT ALL... PSYCHOLOGISTS CALL IT A FREE-FLOATING ANXIETY
GARFIELD
© 1979 PAWS, INC. All Rights Reserved.

SPLAT!
FREE-FLOAT THIS!
GARFIELD
4-13

I WONDER IF THIS EVER HAPPENED TO FREUD
GARFIELD
JIM DAVIS

EASY, BOYS
© 1979 PAWS, INC. All Rights Reserved.

WE LOVE YOU, GARFIELD!

DARN. THAT WAS THE BEST DEEP BLUE FUNK I EVER HAD GOING
4-14
JIM DAVIS

GARFIELD®

SCRATCH
SCRATCH
SCRATCH

SCRATCH
SCRATCH
SCRATCH

PAT
PAT
PAT

SCRATCH
SCRATCH
PAT
PAT
© 1979 PAWS, INC. All Rights Reserved.
4-15

SCRATCH
SCRATCH
PAT
PAT

SCRATCH
PAT

YIP!
ROWR!
BARK!

I DON'T THINK
I COULD TAKE
MUCH MORE
LOVING
JIM DAVIS

LET'S GO CHECK THE MAILBOX, GARFIELD
© 1979 PAWS, INC. All Rights Reserved.

I LOVE GETTING MAIL
4-16

JIM DAVIS
IT'S JUST ANOTHER REMINDER YOU'RE ALIVE
THAT'S A PRETTY HEAVY THOUGHT FOR A MONDAY

HOW ABOUT SOME BOILED CABBAGE FOR LUNCH, GARFIELD?
4-17

SWIPE!

OR MAYBE SOME COLESLAW
NOW YOU'RE TALKING
JIM DAVIS
© 1979 PAWS, INC. All Rights Reserved.

ARF! ARF! ARF!
4-18

SAD
YIP!
© 1979 PAWS, INC. All Rights Reserved.
JIM DAVIS

'ATTA BOY, GARFIELD!
SQUEAK!
4-19

GO GET 'IM!
SQUEAK!
© 1979 PAWS, INC. All Rights Reserved.

JIM DAVIS
TAKE FIVE, LITTLE BUDDY. WE'LL MAKE ANOTHER PASS IN A FEW MINUTES
PUFF PUFF

HEE HEE
4-20

HA! HA! HA! HA!
POOR LYMAN

HE WOULDN'T BE LAUGHING SO HARD IF HE KNEW ODIE JUST DRANK OUT OF THE TOILET
© 1979 PAWS, INC. All Rights Reserved.
JIM DAVIS

HMMM
© 1979 PAWS, INC. All Rights Reserved.
4-21

JIM DAVIS

GARFIELD®

HMMMM

HERE, ODIE
4-22

YIP!
YIP!
YIP!
JIM DAVIS

GARFIELD! GET OUT OF MY SOCK DRAWER!

4-23
© 1979 PAWS, INC. All Rights Reserved.

CRASH!

IT'S AMAZING THE FUN YOU CAN HAVE WITH A HOOP
JIM DAVIS

GEE, I'D ALMOST FORGOTTEN HOW MUCH FUN IT IS TO HANG ON THE OLD SCREEN DOOR
4-24

© 1979 PAWS, INC. All Rights Reserved.
SLAM!

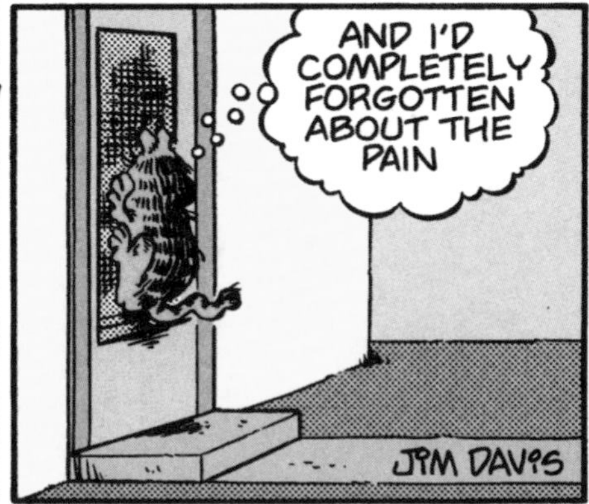
AND I'D COMPLETELY FORGOTTEN ABOUT THE PAIN
JIM DAVIS

HMMM A WHISTLE
© 1979 PAWS, INC. All Rights Reserved.

MUST BE BROKEN
JIM DAVIS
4-25

© 1979 PAWS, INC. All Rights Reserved.
CLAWS ARE GREAT
4-26

THEY ALLOW US CATS TO WALK RIGHT UP TREES

THERE'S ONLY ONE PROBLEM
JIM DAVIS

© 1979 PAWS, INC. All Rights Reserved.
4-27

POP
T

THEY DON'T CALL ME "LIGHTNING LIPS" FOR NOTHING
JIM DAVIS

I JUST WANT YOU PEOPLE TO KNOW HOW MUCH WE CATS APPRECIATE YOU. WITHOUT YOU, WHO WOULD FEED US? WHO WOULD LOVE US?
4-28

AND MOST IMPORTANT OF ALL...

WHO WOULD CHANGE OUR KITTY LITTER?
JIM DAVIS
© 1979 PAWS, INC. All Rights Reserved.

GARFIELD®

GROWL

THE CAT CRAVES FRESH MEAT
4-29

WHAT-HO, THE CAT SENSES UNSUSPECTING QUARRY O'ER YON KNOLL
© 1979 PAWS, INC. All Rights Reserved.
JIM DAVIS

COILING LIKE A SPRING, HE PREPARES TO LUNGE

STEELY SINEWS PROPEL HIM TOWARD HIS HELPLESS PREY

ONCE AGAIN A CAT'S PRIMAL INSTINCTS PROVIDE SUSTENANCE

BOY, I'M STARVED. I THINK I'LL HAVE SAUSAGE, HASH BROWNS AND SOME EGGS OVER EASY
4-30

GOOD MORNING, GARFIELD. HERE'S TUNA AND LIVER SURPRISE!
GARFI

THE SAUSAGE AND HASH BROWNS ARE DELICIOUS. BUT I DO BELIEVE THE EGGS ARE A BIT OVER-DONE
GARFIELD
JIM DAVIS
© 1979 PAWS, INC. All Rights Reserved.

GASP! CHOKE!

BRACK! COUGH! HACK!

FLOP!
ARFIELD
5-1

CAN THE MELODRAMATICS, GARFIELD, AND FINISH YOUR LIVER
JIM DAVIS
© 1979 PAWS, INC. All Rights Reserved.

BURP!
GARFIELD
5-2

THAT WAS RUDE AND CRUDE, GARFIELD. CATS ARE MORE SOPHISTICATED THAN TO SUBMIT TO BELCHING AT THE DINNER TABLE
GARFIELD

BRAACK!
GARFIELD
JIM DAVIS
© 1979 PAWS, INC. All Rights Reserved.

TELL ME WHAT YOU THINK OF MY NEW POEM, GARFIELD
5-3

"MY BUDDY"
I HAVE A BUDDY.
MY BUDDY'S A TOAD.
HE'S KIND OF MUDDY,
HE'S FLAT ON THE ROAD.
BUT, HE IS MY BUDDY,
MY BUDDY TO STAY.
'TIL HE'S PEELED UP
AND SAILED AWAY

GARFIELD?
JIM DAVIS
© 1979 PAWS, INC. All Rights Reserved.

© 1979 PAWS, INC. All Rights Reserved.
5-4

UH-OH, HERE COMES JON!

JIM DAVIS

ARE YOU HUNGRY, ODIE?
© 1979 PAWS, INC. All Rights Reserved.

HERE, HAVE SOME CELERY AND TOMATOES AND RADISHES

GARFIELD!
5-5
JIM DAVIS

GARFIELD®

PURRRR

PURRR

TAPPITY
TAPPITY
TAPPITY
TAPPITY
TAPPITY
TAPPITY

© 1979 PAWS, INC. All Rights Reserved.
5-6

SCRATCH!
SCRATCH!
SCRATCH!
SCRATCH!

GOOD MORNING, SUNSHINE. WELCOME TO ANOTHER GLORIOUS, FUN-FILLED DAY WITH YOUR FAVORITE PET!

I'M SO HAPPY TO OWN A CAT, I COULD JUST THROW UP
JIM DAVIS

HEY, LYMAN. WHERE'S MY BREAD KNIFE?
© 1979 PAWS, INC. All Rights Reserved.
5-7

SLASH!

NEVER MIND
JIM DAVIS

THIS IS TOO GOOD TO BE TRUE
© 1979 PAWS, INC. All Rights Reserved.

BOING!

THAT **WAS** TOO GOOD TO BE TRUE
JIM DAVIS
5-8

GOBBLE! GOBBLE!
JIM DAVIS

WITH ALL RESPECT TO WILL ROGERS
5-9

I NEVER MET A LASAGNA I DIDN'T LIKE
© 1979 PAWS, INC. All Rights Reserved.

5-10
CRASH!

UH-OH ! HERE COMES JON
© 1979 PAWS, INC. All Rights Reserved.

JIM DAVIS

HELLO, JULIE ? HOW ABOUT A MOVIE TONIGHT ? OH, I SEE. OKAY, GOODBYE
© 1979 PAWS, INC. All Rights Reserved.

DARN, SHE SAID SHE WAS JUST WALKING OUT THE DOOR TO VISIT HER BROTHER IN TOKYO
CLICK
5-11

THAT'S WHAT I CALL BAD TIMING
THAT'S CALLED GETTING SHOT OUT OF THE SADDLE, YOU TURKEY
JIM DAVIS

GARFIELD, YOU'RE GETTING TOO FAT
5-12

I AM **NOT** GETTING TOO FAT

I'M JUST READY FOR THE NEXT SIZE KITTY BED, THAT'S ALL
© 1979 PAWS, INC. All Rights Reserved.
JIM DAVIS

THIS CAT FOOD IS MADE OF:
DRIED WHEY, SODIUM CASEINATE, ISOLATED SOY PROTEIN, CALCIUM CARBONATE, PHOSPHORIC ACID, DICALCIUM PHOSPHATE, CORN GLUTEN MEAL, WHEAT GERM MEAL, BREWER'S DRIED YEAST, IODIZED SALT, GROUND WHEAT, GROUND CORN, SOYBEAN MEAL, POULTRY BY-PRODUCT MEAL, ANIMAL FAT PRESERVED WITH BHA, WHEAT GERM MEAL, CHOLINE CHLORIDE, CITRIC ACID, ONION POWDER, THIAMIN, PARA AMINOBENZOIC ACID, RIBOFLAVIN SUPPLEMENT, MENADIONE SODIUM BISULFITE, CALCIUM PANTOTHENATE

MUNCHIES

BOY, WHAT A GREAT MEAL

UH-OH!

5-14
GARFIELD
© 1979 PAWS, INC. All Rights Reserved.
JIM DAVIS

IT WAS BOUND TO HAPPEN. MY STOMACH FINALLY OUTGREW MY LEGS
© 1979 PAWS, INC. All Rights Reserved.
5-15

WORSE THINGS COULD HAPPEN, I GUESS

LIKE THIS, FOR INSTANCE
JIM DAVIS

WELL, YOU'VE FINALLY DONE IT, GARFIELD. YOUR BELLY'S BIGGER THAN YOUR LEGS. NOW WHAT ARE YOU GOING TO DO?
© 1979 PAWS, INC. All Rights Reserved.
5-16

I'LL SHOW YOU WHAT I'M GOING TO DO

IF YOU'LL JUST ROLL ME OVER TO THAT LASAGNA THERE
JIM DAVIS

YOU'RE GOING TO HAVE TO EXERCISE THAT BELLY OFF, GARFIELD
© 1979 PAWS, INC. All Rights Reserved.

TELL YOU WHAT. I'LL GET A LEASH AND TAKE YOU FOR A BRISK MORNING DRAG

IF HE HAD A BRAIN, I'D SAY HE WAS TRYING TO MAKE A FUNNY
5-17
JIM DAVIS

© 1979 PAWS, INC. All Rights Reserved.
5-18

BOING
BOING
BO
JIM DAVIS

AT LAST! MY FEET CAN TOUCH THE FLOOR ONCE MORE
JIM DAVIS
5-19

NEVER AGAIN WILL I ALLOW MYSELF TO GET THAT FAT
© 1979 PAWS, INC. All Rights Reserved.

AND IF YOU BELIEVE THAT, I HAVE A BRIDGE TO SELL YOU

GARFIELD®

RIDE 'EM, COWCAT!

BONK!
5-20
© 1979 PAWS, INC. All Rights Reserved.

OH, NO! ODIE'S HURT HIS LEG! WHAT'LL I DO?
SHOOT HIM
JIM DAVIS

I THINK IT'S TIME WE TAKE GARFIELD AND ODIE OUT FOR SOMETHING TO DO
5-21

WHY DO YOU SAY THAT?

THEY'RE TAKING TURNS ON THE RECORD PLAYER AGAIN
JIM DAVIS
© 1979 PAWS, INC. All Rights Reserved.

CATS CAN BE VERY CURIOUS
ATSUP
5-22

SPLOOCH!
ATSUP

CATS CAN ALSO BE VERY STUPID
© 1979 PAWS, INC. All Rights Reserved.
JIM DAVIS

DID I EVER TELL YOU ABOUT MY UNCLE HARRY? HE WAS A FAMOUS MOUSER AT A GLASS PLANT IN GAS CITY, INDIANA
5-23
© 1979 PAWS, INC. All Rights Reserved.

LEGEND HAS IT THAT UNCLE HARRY CHASED A MOUSE RIGHT INTO TANK #2

NOW HE'S A PAPERWEIGHT IN BAYONNE, NEW JERSEY
JIM DAVIS

GRAB!
JIM DAVIS
© 1979 PAWS, INC. All Rights Reserved.

BONK!

SMOOTH MOVE, OL' BUDDY
HAVE YOU NO RESPECT FOR THE DEAD?
5-24

HELLO, CAROLYN? HEY, HOW ABOUT TAKING IN A MOVIE TONIGHT? UH... OH SURE, I UNDERSTAND

SHE SAID SHE WOULD LOVE TO HAVE GONE OUT WITH ME TONIGHT
CLICK
JIM DAVIS
© 1979 PAWS, INC. All Rights Reserved.

BUT SHE HAD TO STAY HOME AND PLUCK HER EYEBROWS
SUBTLE
5-25

THE DARN LAWN MOWER WON'T WORK
LET ME TRY

© 1979 PAWS, INC. All Rights Reserved.

IF I COULD PACKAGE THAT LOOK, I'D MAKE A MILLION
BRRR!
5-26
JIM DAVIS

GARFIELD®

DING DONG
—TUG TUG

GOOD EVENING, FELICIA, MY DEAR. DINNER AWAITS

A LOAF OF BREAD, A JUG OF WINE AND THOU (HEH-HEH)
OH, BROTHER

© 1979 PAWS, INC. All Rights Reserved.

WAHCHOO!

I'M ALLERGIC TO CATS! EITHER HE GOES OR I GO
SNIFF!
5-27

POOMP!

GEE, AND SHE WAS CUTE, TOO
SALUD
JIM DAVIS

OH, GOODY. IT'S MONDAY MORNING
BRING!
© 1979 PAWS, INC. All Rights Reserved.

I LOVE MONDAY MORNINGS. YOU KNOW WHY?

BECAUSE **I** DON'T HAVE TO GO TO WORK
5-28
JIM DAVIS

AH, SIX A.M. TIME TO RISE AND SHINE
BRING!
© 1979 PAWS, INC. All Rights Reserved.

FIRST, A LIGHT BREAKFAST OF JUICE AND TOAST, THEN SOME JOGGING

HA-HA-HA! THAT WAS A GOOD ONE
5-29
JIM DAVIS

Z
© 1979 PAWS, INC. All Rights Reserved.

Z
SMACK
SMACK

OH MY GOSH! I SLEPT THROUGH TODAY'S STRIP!
5-30
JIM DAVIS

THERE'S ONLY ONE DRAWBACK TO SPENDING A WEEK IN BED...
© 1979 PAWS, INC. All Rights Reserved.

SNIFF!

THIS BLANKET IS STARTING TO DEVELOP A PERSONALITY ALL ITS OWN
5-31
JIM DAVIS

GARFIELD, YOU'VE BEEN IN BED ALL WEEK. WHY, YOU COULD STARVE TO DEATH
© 1979 PAWS, INC. All Rights Reserved.

OH

I SHOULD HAVE GUESSED AS MUCH
6-1
JIM DAVIS

GET OUT OF BED THIS MINUTE, GARFIELD
JIM DAVIS
6-2

GOOD BOY!
DARN LEG CRAMPS
© 1979 PAWS, INC. All Rights Reserved.

GARFIELD®

PTOOEY!

PTOOEY!
6-3
JIM DAVIS

PTOOEY!

OKAY, GARFIELD. NOW GIVE ME SOME HIGH LOBS
© 1979 PAWS, INC. All Rights Reserved.

HAVE A PACKAGE OF CRACKERS, GARFIELD
© 1979 PAWS, INC. All Rights Reserved.

RUSTLE
CRACKLE
CRINKLE

THEY WERE TERRIBLE!
NEXT TIME TRY TAKING THEM OUT OF THE WRAPPER
6-4
JIM DAVIS

WHY THE DROOPY DEMEANOR TODAY, GARFIELD?
© 1979 PAWS, INC. All Rights Reserved.
6-5

KONK!

NEVER SAY "DROOP" TO A FAT PERSON
JIM DAVIS

HEY, LYMAN. WHAT DO YOU THINK OF MY NEW TENNIS RACKET?

WHAT'S IT STRUNG WITH?
CATGUT
6-6

© 1979 PAWS, INC. All Rights Reserved.
AUNT REBA!
JIM DAVIS

THAT'S THE TROUBLE WITH WARM WEATHER
JIM DAVIS

YOU CAN'T KEEP ICE CUBES IN YOUR DRINK

© 1979 PAWS, INC. All Rights Reserved.
6-7

TOUCH MY PIE AND YOU DIE
© 1979 PAWS, INC. All Rights Reserved.

TOUCH

ALWAYS RIDING THE RAGGED EDGE OF DISASTER, AREN'T YOU, GARFIELD?!
ZOOM!!!
JIM DAVIS
6-8

WAITRESS, THIS POTATO IS BAD
© 1979 PAWS, INC. All Rights Reserved.

BAD POTATO! BAD POTATO!
SMACK! SMACK! SMACK!

6-9
SIR, IF THAT POTATO GIVES YOU ANY MORE TROUBLE, YOU JUST LET ME KNOW
THERE GOES HER TIP
JIM DAVIS

GARFIELD®

IT'S ONLY NOON, GARFIELD. WHY DON'T YOU SLEEP IN TODAY. YOU DESERVE THE REST

HEY, GARFIELD! LET'S HAVE SOME FUN! I'LL HOLD ODIE DOWN AND YOU BEAT HIM UP

HOW ABOUT SOME EXERCISE, GARFIELD? WHY DON'T YOU SCRATCH UP MY FAVORITE CHAIR HERE?
6-10
© 1979 PAWS, INC. All Rights Reserved.

DON'T WORRY ABOUT KNOCKING THE PLANTS OFF THE SHELF TODAY, GARFIELD. WE'LL DO IT FOR YOU
CRASH!
CRASH!

I BAKED TONS OF LASAGNA FOR YOU OL' BUDDY. **EAT! EAT!**

POOF!

WHAT A DEPRESSING DREAM. FOR A MOMENT THERE I THOUGHT ALL THE FUN HAD GONE OUT OF MY LIFE
JIM DAVIS

COME ON, GARFIELD. LET'S GO CAMPING
NOT ON YOUR LIFE
© 1979 PAWS, INC. All Rights Reserved.
JIM DAVIS

GEE, AND I'D PACKED LOTS OF LASAGNA, TOO

SINCE YOU PUT IT THAT WAY, I RECKON THERE'S A TRAIL OR TWO OUT THERE THAT COULD STAND A LITTLE BLAZING
6-11

WELL, HERE WE ARE IN THE GREAT OUTDOORS, GARFIELD

AH, WILDERNESS

JUST US, THE SKY, AND THE TREES
WHERE'S THE TV?
© 1979 PAWS, INC. All Rights Reserved.
6-12
JIM DAVIS

WELL, GARFIELD
© 1979 PAWS, INC. All Rights Reserved.

WHAT DO YOU THINK OF CAMPING SO FAR?
I DON'T KNOW

I'VE NEVER BEEN THIS FAR FROM THE SANDBOX BEFORE
6-13
JIM DAVIS

WHY THE LONG FACE, GARFIELD?
6-14

LOOK WHO I BROUGHT
POOKY!

© 1979 PAWS, INC. All Rights Reserved.
CAMPING IS MORE FUN WITH A GOOD FRIEND
JIM DAVIS

© 1979 PAWS, INC. All Rights Reserved.

WHAT'S THAT ?

MUST BE A PORCUPINE
6-15
JIM DAVIS

GARFIELD! YOU'RE COVERED WITH PORCUPINE QUILLS!
6-16
© 1979 PAWS, INC. All Rights Reserved.

THAT MUST BE VERY PAINFUL
I CAN HANDLE IT

ARRRRRGH!
JIM DAVIS

GARFIELD®

SCREW
SCREW
SCREW

LOOK, GARFIELD! I MADE A KITTY DOOR FOR YOU

SWING

SMACK!
© 1979 PAWS, INC. All Rights Reserved.

SMASH!

A CLEAR-CUT CASE OF SELF-DEFENSE IF I EVER SAW ONE
JIM DAVIS
6-17

WHAT WOULD YOU LIKE FOR YOUR BIRTHDAY, GARFIELD ?
ANOTHER SCRATCHING POST
6-18

HOW ABOUT A NICE RUBBER MOUSIE ?
© 1979 PAWS, INC. All Rights Reserved.

OR MAYBE ANOTHER SCRATCHING POST
HOW'D YOU GUESS ?
JIM DAVIS

HAPPY FIRST BIRTHDAY, GARFIELD! MAKE A WISH AND BLOW OUT THE CANDLE
6-19

FOOF!
© 1979 PAWS, INC. All Rights Reserved.

OH GEE. THAT'S TOO BAD
NOT REALLY. I GOT MY WISH
JIM DAVIS

HAVE A SAUSAGE
6-20

© 1979 PAWS, INC. All Rights Reserved.

ONE AT A TIME, GARFIELD, ONE AT A TIME
JIM DAVIS

HERE'S TO GLUTTONY!
GARFIELD
© 1979 PAWS, INC. All Rights Reserved.

GULP!
ARFIELD

HELLO? OVEREATERS ANONYMOUS?
JIM DAVIS
6-21

HELLO, VALETTE? HEY, HOW ABOUT MEETING ME SOME-WHERE TONIGHT, SWEETS?
6-22

YOU'LL MEET ME WHEN **WHAT** FREEZES OVER?
© 1979 PAWS, INC. All Rights Reserved.

I CAN TAKE A HINT
ONLY IF IT'S APPLIED WITH A SLEDGEHAMMER
SLAM!
JIM DAVIS

DO YOU KNOW WHY I DON'T CHASE BIRDS? WELL, I'LL TELL YOU
6-23

MY UNCLE HUBERT ONCE CAUGHT A 30-POUND CANARY IN CHICAGO
© 1979 PAWS, INC. All Rights Reserved.

THEY LAST SPOTTED HIM OVER DALLAS, TEXAS
JIM DAVIS

GARFIELD®

HOW ABOUT A SNACK, GARFIELD?

HERE'S SOME LIVER LEFT FROM DINNER
BLECH!
6-24

IT'S GOOD. REALLY. WATCH ME

M-M-M-M NUMMY, NUMMY, NUMMY
OH, VERY WELL
© 1979 PAWS, INC. All Rights Reserved.

A MOUSE! GET IT!

GARFIELD, WHY CAN'T YOU CHASE MICE LIKE OTHER CATS?

IF JON EATS ONE FIRST, I'LL CONSIDER IT
JIM DAVIS

I'M GOING TO TAKE YOU TO THE VET FOR A CHECKUP, GARFIELD
OH-NO!
6-25

MY UNCLE BARNEY WENT TO THE VET ONCE

HE CAME BACK AS MY AUNT BERNICE
JIM DAVIS
© 1979 PAWS, INC. All Rights Reserved.

THE DOCTOR WILL SEE YOUR CAT IN A MOMENT
6-26

WHO'S NEXT, PLEASE?

I THINK I JUST DIED AND WENT TO HEAVEN
I THINK I JUST DIED
JIM DAVIS
© 1979 PAWS, INC. All Rights Reserved.

BY THE WAY THERE, DOC, WHAT'S YOUR NAME?
LIZ
© 1979 PAWS, INC. All Rights Reserved.

GEE, WHAT A PRETTY NAME. IS THAT SHORT FOR ELIZABETH?
NO. IT'S SHORT FOR LIZARD

LIZ MUST NOT BE MUCH FOR SMALL TALK
6-27
JIM DAVIS

I GUESS WE'LL BE SEEING A LOT OF EACH OTHER, DOC. GARFIELD GETS SICK A LOT. DON'T YOU, GARFIELD?
JIM DAVIS

DON'T YOU, GARFIELD?

© 1979 PAWS, INC. All Rights Reserved.
KACHEW
KACHEW
6-28

WELL, MR. ARBUCKLE, YOUR CAT'S BASICALLY IN GOOD HEALTH

BUT YOU'LL HAVE TO TAKE BETTER CARE OF HIM
LISTEN TO THE DOCTOR, JON
6-29

HE'S TOO FAT
CLOSE YOUR EARS, BOY! THE WOMAN'S SOME KIND OF A QUACK!
JIM DAVIS
© 1979 PAWS, INC. All Rights Reserved.

TELL ME, LIZ, HAVEN'T WE MET SOMEWHERE BEFORE? A RICE PADDY IN HONG KONG?
6-30

LOOK, JERK. I'LL BE THE VET FOR YOUR CAT, BUT I WON'T PLAY FALL GUY FOR YOUR STUPID LINES. UNDERSTOOD?
UH-HUH

SO LONG, DOCTOR
HAVE A NICE DAY
© 1979 PAWS, INC. All Rights Reserved.
JIM DAVIS

GARFIELD®

BARK!

POW!
POW!

CRACK!

CRASH!

GRRRR

THEY DON'T TELL YOU ABOUT THESE THINGS IN THE PET MAGAZINES
JIM DAVIS
7-1

YOU'RE TOO FAT, GARFIELD
7-2

WHY, I'LL BET YOU HAVEN'T SEEN YOUR FEET IN YEARS

I HAVE FEET?
JIM DAVIS
© 1979 PAWS, INC. All Rights Reserved.

CRUNCH
JIM DAVIS

I THINK IT'S TIME I PUT YOU ON ANOTHER DIET, GARFIELD

WHATEVER GAVE HIM THAT IDEA?
7-3
© 1979 PAWS, INC. All Rights Reserved.

I'M STARTING YOUR DIET, GARFIELD
7-4
© 1979 PAWS, INC. All Rights Reserved.

HOW WOULD YOU LIKE THIS HEAD OF CABBAGE PREPARED?
DEEP-FRY THAT SUCKER

BOILED IT IS
WHAT WE HAVE HERE IS A FAILURE TO COMMUNICATE
JIM DAVIS

HMMM, DIET CANDY
CANDY
7-5
© 1979 PAWS, INC. All Rights Reserved.

NOT BAD

A COUPLE MORE BOXES OF THOSE THINGS AND I'LL BE SKINNIER THAN A RAIL
JIM DAVIS

THIS DIET I'M ON HAS SURE MADE ME WEAK
© 1979 PAWS, INC. All Rights Reserved.
7-6

PUNT!

DRAT, HE USUALLY CLEARS THE PIANO
JIM DAVIS

I WONDER WHAT I'D LOOK LIKE SKINNY?
© 1979 PAWS, INC. All Rights Reserved.

GARFIELD! YOUR DIET!
MY VANITY
JIM DAVIS 7-7

GARFIELD®

FOOD!

WHAT'S THIS ?

IT APPEARS TO BE OF THE CRESCENT ROLL FAMILY

A TRUE GOURMET NEVER SHIES AWAY FROM A NEW TASTE TREAT

(SMACK) A BIT DRY, BUT PALATABLE

GARFIELD, HAVE YOU SEEN MY SWEAT SOCKS?
JIM DAVIS
7-8

© 1979 PAWS, INC. All Rights Reserved.
CATS ARE THE WORLD'S GREATEST TREE CLIMBERS

THERE'S ONLY ONE TINY PROBLEM...

CATS ARE ALSO THE WORLD'S WORST TREE CLIMBER DOWNERS
7/9
JIM DAVIS

I'VE MADE UP MY MIND. THE ONLY WAY OUT OF THIS TREE IS TO JUMP. I MAY BREAK EVERY BONE IN MY BODY, BUT HERE GOES
© 1979 PAWS, INC. All Rights Reserved.

THEN AGAIN...
7-10
JIM DAVIS

CATCH THE ROPE, GARFIELD!

© 1979 PAWS, INC. All Rights Reserved.
NOW TIE IT AROUND YOUR WAIST AND I'LL PULL YOU DOWN. HA-HA-HA!

I'LL GET JON FOR THAT
7-11
JIM DAVIS

I'VE COME TO RESCUE YOU, GARFIELD
JIM DAVIS

UH-OH

WELL, THIS IS JUST DUCKY
7-12
© 1979 PAWS, INC. All Rights Reserved.

THERE'S ONLY ONE WAY OUT OF THIS TREE, GARFIELD
7-13
JIM DAVIS

WE'LL HAVE TO JUMP

GEE, I'D LOVE TO BUT I SIMPLY HAVEN'T A THING TO WEAR TO OUR FUNERAL
© 1979 PAWS, INC. All Rights Reserved.

EITHER WE JUMP, OR WE'LL STARVE UP HERE, GARFIELD
I'M WITH YOU
JIM DAVIS

GERONIMO!!

© 1979 PAWS, INC. All Rights Reserved.
7-14

GARFIELD®

AHEM... ME, ME, MEEE

♪ MEYOWRRR ♫
7-15

BONK

I WONDER IF THIS IS HOW ENRICO CARUSO GOT HIS START
© 1979 PAWS, INC. All Rights Reserved.

♪ MEYOWRRRR ♫

CLOBBER!!

CLINK
CLINK
CLANK

♪ MEYOWRR ♫
BINK
JIM DAVIS

ZOOM!
© 1979 PAWS, INC. All Rights Reserved.
7-16

WHY, OH WHY, OH WHY, OH WHY, DO CATS DO THESE THINGS?
JIM DAVIS

I'M GETTING OUT OF THIS TREE IF IT KILLS ME
7-17

POOMP!

GEE, THAT DIDN'T HURT AT ALL
© 1979 PAWS, INC. All Rights Reserved.
JIM DAVIS

WHAT ARE YOU DOING WITH THE ICE PICK, GARFIELD?
© 1979 PAWS, INC. All Rights Reserved.
7-18

STAB
STAB
STAB
STAB
STAB

THE ONLY WAY TO EAT PEAS
OH
JIM DAVIS

WELL, HELLO THERE, GOOD-LOOKING
© 1979 PAWS, INC. All Rights Reserved.
7-19

SAY, WHAT'RE YOU DOING TONIGHT ?

HOW ABOUT COMING TO MY PLACE FOR DINNER ?
JIM DAVIS

SAY, HOW ABOUT POPPING OVER TO MY PLACE FOR A LATE-NIGHT SNACK?
© 1979 PAWS, INC. All Rights Reserved.
7-20

HA-HA-HA. YOU NEEDN'T BE AFRAID OF LITTLE OL' ME

IF YOU LIKE, YOU CAN BRING A FRIEND AND WE'LL HAVE DESSERT, TOO
JIM DAVIS

I'M SORRY. WE DON'T SERVE CATS HERE
© 1979 PAWS, INC. All Rights Reserved.

WHAT WILL YOU AND YOUR DOG HAVE, SIR ?
7-21
JIM DAVIS

GARFIELD®

GO GET 'IM, GARFIELD!

© 1979 PAWS, INC. All Rights Reserved.

OOPS!
SQUEAK!

EVERYONE STAND BACK! GIVE HIM SOME AIR!

ARTIFICIAL RESPIRATION MIGHT HELP
7-22

OKAY, GO, BOY

PHEW! FOR A MINUTE THERE I THOUGHT I WAS OUT OF A JOB
JIM DAVIS

COME ON, GARFIELD. LET'S GO SEE YOUR VET
© 1979 PAWS, INC. All Rights Reserved.
7-23

SHE SURE IS CUTE

WHY IS IT EVERY TIME **HE** GETS A HOT FLASH, **I** HAVE TO GO TO THE DOCTOR ?
JIM DAVIS

HOW ABOUT A DATE, DOC ?
I'D SOONER DIE
JIM DAVIS

WELL DON'T DO **THAT**
© 1979 PAWS, INC. All Rights Reserved.

NOTHING LIKE A SNAPPY COMEBACK TO SAVE FACE
7-24

HOW ABOUT A DATE, SWEETHEART ?
© 1979 PAWS, INC. All Rights Reserved.
JIM DAVIS

THAT'S **DOCTOR** TO YOU
7-25

OKAY, HOW ABOUT A DATE, **DOCTOR** SWEETHEART ?

TELL ME, DOC
© 1979 PAWS, INC. All Rights Reserved.

DO YOU MAKE HOUSE CALLS?
7-26

IT'S NOT THE VETERINARY MEDICINE I MIND. IT'S SOME OF THE ANIMALS I HAVE TO WORK WITH
JIM DAVIS

© 1979 PAWS, INC. All Rights Reserved.

TELL ME, DOCTOR, WHAT DO YOU SUGGEST FOR AN ANIMAL WHO'S MADLY IN LOVE?
JIM DAVIS

I USUALLY PRESCRIBE NEUTERING
7-27

WE'LL MAKE AN APPOINTMENT FOR GARFIELD'S NEXT CHECK-UP IN ABOUT SIX MONTHS
7-28
JIM DAVIS

WHAT IF THERE'S AN EMERGENCY?
THEN YOU CAN CALL ME DAY OR NIGHT
© 1979 PAWS, INC. All Rights Reserved.

COME ON, GARFIELD. LET'S GO HOME AND PLAY IN TRAFFIC
THAT'S NOT FUNNY

GARFIELD®

CRASH!
7-29

SMASH!
© 1979 PAWS, INC. All Rights Reserved.

LEAP!

SPLAT!

TAKE THAT!
JIM DAVIS

7-30

ZOOM!

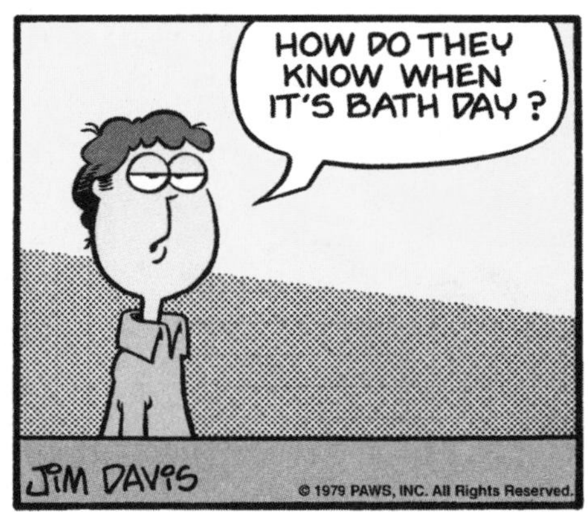
HOW DO THEY KNOW WHEN IT'S BATH DAY?
JIM DAVIS
© 1979 PAWS, INC. All Rights Reserved.

BATH TIME!
© 1979 PAWS, INC. All Rights Reserved.
7-31

CHUCKLE CHUCKLE
SOAP

OKAY, WHO PUT OATMEAL IN THE SOAPBOX?
WELL, SPRINKLE ME WITH BROWN SUGAR AND CALL ME FOR BREAKFAST
JIM DAVIS

WHY CAN'T YOU BE LIKE OTHER CATS, GARFIELD?
JIM DAVIS
8-1

LET ME EXPLAIN THE BASIC DIFFERENCES BETWEEN HUMANS AND CATS

WELL, MAKE IT SNAPPY. I HAVE A TENNIS LESSON IN HALF AN HOUR
© 1979 PAWS, INC. All Rights Reserved.

TIME FOR A MIDNIGHT SNACK
CEREAL
8-2
© 1979 PAWS, INC. All Rights Reserved.

CRINKLE
CEREAL

CEREAL
JIM DAVIS

BOING
BOING
BOING
8-3

NG
BOING
BOING

HELP!
BOING
BOING
© 1979 PAWS, INC. All Rights Reserved.
JIM DAVIS

FOR STAYING OUT OF MY FOOD TODAY, GARFIELD, I'M GOING TO REWARD YOU WITH A KITTY MUNCHIE
KITTY MUNCHIE
© 1979 PAWS, INC. All Rights Reserved.

8-4

THEY'RE GONE
I ALREADY REWARDED MYSELF
JIM DAVIS

GARFIELD®

8-5

© 1979 PAWS, INC. All Rights Reserved.

WHAT SAY I SWITCH OVER TO THE MOVIE, GANG?

NAH
GRRR
FFFT

JIM DAVIS

GARFIELD'S HISTORY OF CATS:
THE VERY FIRST CAT CRAWLED OUT OF THE SEA ABOUT TEN MILLION YEARS AGO
8-6

FORTUNATELY FOR HIM...

IT WAS ONLY ABOUT ANOTHER 15 MINUTES BEFORE THE FIRST MOUSE CRAWLED OUT
JIM DAVIS
© 1979 PAWS, INC. All Rights Reserved.

GARFIELD'S HISTORY OF CATS:
THE FIRST CAT WAS DOMESTICATED ABOUT A MILLION YEARS AGO. THE CAT (NAMED "ORG") WAS OWNED BY A CAVE MAN NAMED "CHUCK"
8-7

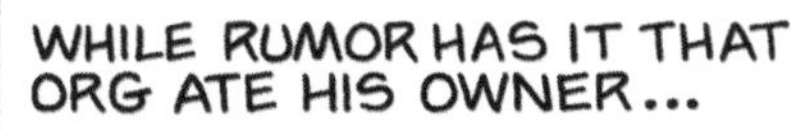
WHILE RUMOR HAS IT THAT ORG ATE HIS OWNER...

© 1979 PAWS, INC. All Rights Reserved.

HISTORIANS MAINTAIN THE FAMILY DOG ATE CHUCK
JIM DAVIS

GARFIELD'S HISTORY OF CATS:
DURING THE DARK AGES THE LEGENDARY RATTER "FLUFFY-THE-FIERCE" DESTROYED EVERY RAT BUT ONE...
SQUEAK!
JIM DAVIS

OL' FLUFFY GOT HIS CLOCK CLEANED BY THE EVEN MORE LEGENDARY "MATT-THE-RAT"
DRIBBLE
DRIBBLE
DRIBBLE

INCIDENTALLY, IT WAS MATT-THE-RAT WHO COINED THE TERM "HERE, KITTY, KITTY, KITTY"
© 1979 PAWS, INC. All Rights Reserved.
8-8

GARFIELD'S HISTORY OF CATS:
MARCO POLO HAD A CAT NAMED ROLO
ROLO POLO
8-9

ROLO WOULD HAVE GONE WITH MARCO ON HIS TRIP TO THE ORIENT...

BUT MOTELS WOULDN'T ACCEPT PETS THEN
WAH!
JIM DAVIS

GARFIELD'S HISTORY OF CATS:
A CAT DISCOVERED AMERICA!

IT WAS CHRISTOPHER COLUMBUS' CAT "BUCKEYE" WHO FIRST SPOTTED THE BEACH

PRIMARILY BECAUSE THE SANTA MARIA DIDN'T HAVE A SANDBOX
8-10
JIM DAVIS

GARFIELD'S HISTORY OF CATS:
CATS' PENCHANT FOR SHARPENING THEIR CLAWS HAS SERVED MANY HISTORIC PURPOSES:
IN VICTORIAN TIMES CATS WERE USED TO ANTIQUE FURNITURE
RRRRRRRR
8-11

DURING THE SPANISH-AMERICAN WAR, CATS WERE USED AS INTERROGATORS
I'LL TALK! I'LL TALK!

AND TODAY, THE POST OFFICE USES CATS TO SORT MAIL MARKED "FRAGILE"
JIM DAVIS

GARFIELD®

BOY, IT'S HOT!

CHIRP CHIRP WHEEE!
© 1979 PAWS, INC. All Rights Reserved.

OUT, BIRDS. OUT, OUT, OUT

8-12

SHARKS!

JIM DAVIS

OH, GARFIELD! COME AND...
GARFIELD
8-13
© 1979 PAWS, INC. All Rights Reserved.

ZOOM!

GET IT
GARFIELD
JIM DAVIS

HMMM A DOGGIE BISCUIT
DOGGIE BISCUIT
8-14

WHAT A DISAPPOINTMENT

THAT DOESN'T TASTE AT ALL LIKE DOGGIE
JIM DAVIS
© 1979 PAWS, INC. All Rights Reserved.

ONE THING I ADMIRE IN CATS IS THEIR NATURAL GRACE
© 1979 PAWS, INC. All Rights Reserved.
8-15

SMACK!

AND THEN THERE'S GARFIELD
JIM DAVIS

HMM
8-16

JIM DAVIS
© 1979 PAWS, INC. All Rights Reserved.

YESTERDAY I STUFFED ODIE'S NOSE IN HIS MOUTH
© 1979 PAWS, INC. All Rights Reserved.

YOU SHOULD HAVE SEEN HIM...

RUNNING AROUND IN LITTLE CIRCLES GOING "MARK! MARK! MARK!"
JIM DAVIS
8-17

OH BOY, WHAT A NIGHT. I ATE TOO MUCH, I DRANK TOO MUCH, AND I DANCED HALF THE NIGHT
© 1979 PAWS, INC. All Rights Reserved.

YOU'RE LUCKY YOU'RE A CAT, GARFIELD. YOU DON'T HAVE TO PUT UP WITH ALL THAT

RUB IT IN, WHY DON'T YOU?!
JIM DAVIS
8-18

GARFIELD®

YAWN!
YAWN

LA LA LA ♪
MROW♪
JIM DAVIS

GARFIELD

© 1979 PAWS, INC. All Rights Reserved.

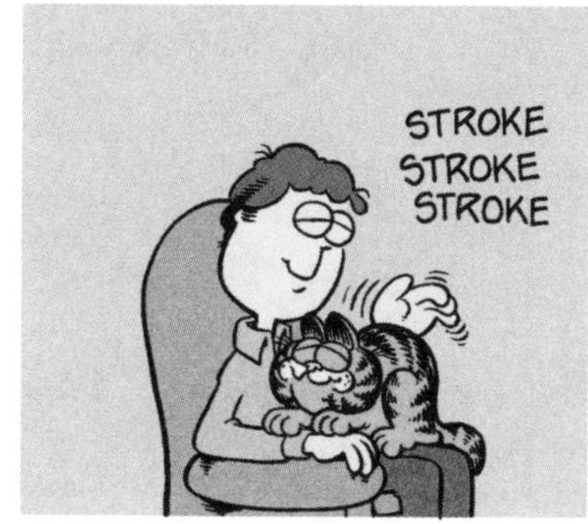
STROKE
STROKE
STROKE

COME ON, GARFIELD. LET'S GO JOGGING
HAVE A GOOD TIME
8-19

HAVE YOU EVER THOUGHT ABOUT MEETING SOME NICE GIRL CAT AND SETTLING DOWN, GARFIELD?
NOT REALLY
8-20

WE BOY CATS CHERISH OUR BACHELORHOOD

WHY, I COME FROM A LONG LINE OF BACHELORS
JIM DAVIS
© 1979 PAWS, INC. All Rights Reserved.

© 1979 PAWS, INC. All Rights Reserved.
8-21

JIM DAVIS

OH, BY THE WAY, GARFIELD

© 1979 PAWS, INC. All Rights Reserved.
CRASH!

8-22
JIM DAVIS
I WAXED THE TV TODAY

HEY, GARFIELD, HOW WOULD YOU LIKE TO GO JOGGING ?
HOW WOULD YOU LIKE ME TO SHRED YOUR SHORTS ?
8-23

SOME NERVE

SHOW ME A JOGGER AND I'LL SHOW YOU A STRANGE PERSON WITH A THING FOR PAIN
© 1979 PAWS, INC. All Rights Reserved.
JIM DAVIS

© 1979 PAWS, INC. All Rights Reserved.
8-24

YOU WIN. YOU WERE UGLIER TO BEGIN WITH
JIM DAVIS

8-25
I'M NEVER TAKING YOU GOLFING AGAIN, GARFIELD
BIG DEAL
© 1979 PAWS, INC. All Rights Reserved.

I'VE NEVER BEEN SO EMBARRASSED

I CAN'T BELIEVE WHAT YOU DID AT THE SEVENTEENTH GREEN
SAND TRAP, SANDBOX, WHAT'S THE DIFFERENCE ?
JIM DAVIS

GARFIELD®

© 1979 PAWS, INC. All Rights Reserved.
WE'RE GOING FOR A WALK, GARFIELD
I **HATE** LEASHES

HEH, HEH. TAKING YOUR PET FOR A STROLL THROUGH THE PARK IS A GREAT WAY TO MEET CHICKS
GRRR FFFT
8-26

ROWRR!

WHAT KIND OF A **JERK** WOULD WALK HIS CAT ON A LEASH?
ROWR!

ROWR! FFFT!
YIP! YIP! YIP!

JIM DAVIS
BACK TO THE DRAWING BOARD

Garfield bigger than life

BY: JIM DAVIS

SAY, YOU LOOK LIKE YOU WANT TO GO JOGGING THIS MORNING, GARFIELD
YOU ARE WRONG, SWEAT SOCK BREATH
8-27

JOGGING IS FINE FOR SOME PEOPLE, I SUPPOSE...

BUT I'VE NEVER BEEN THAT CRAZY ABOUT THE DRY HEAVES
© 1979 PAWS, INC. All Rights Reserved.
JIM DAVIS

KERCHUNK!
8-28

A NEW WORLD'S RECORD
© 1979 PAWS, INC. All Rights Reserved.

WHEN WAS THE LAST TIME YOU STUCK 44 KEYS ON A TYPEWRITER ?
JIM DAVIS

© 1979 PAWS, INC. All Rights Reserved.
8-29

OH, GREAT

GARFIELD ATE MY TOOTHPASTE AGAIN
JIM DAVIS

I JUST LOVE TO COURT DANGER
8-30

SPLOOSH!

YIPEEE, HA-HA, WHEEE
© 1979 PAWS, INC. All Rights Reserved.
JIM DAVIS

THIS IS MY PET ANT, LYLE. HE'S CUTE, QUIET, AND INDUSTRIOUS
8-31
JIM DAVIS

SPLAT!

THE "LATE" LYLE WAS ALSO EYEBALLING MY LASAGNA
© 1979 PAWS, INC. All Rights Reserved.

9-1
© 1979 PAWS, INC. All Rights Reserved.

WHAT ?! WHERE ?!

HE DID IT AGAIN
JIM DAVIS

SCUFFLE
SCUFFLE
STRUGGLE
GRAB!
STUFF
STUFF

GUESS WHAT, GARFIELD? WHILE MOM AND DAD'RE ON A WEEK'S VACATION, WE'RE GOING TO BABY-SIT FOR THEIR KITTEN
9-3

MEET NERMAL

WAKE ME IN A WEEK
© 1979 PAWS, INC. All Rights Reserved.
JIM DAVIS

I GOTTA SPEND A WEEK WET-NURSING NERMAL, HERE... HE'S CUTE
9-4
© 1979 PAWS, INC. All Rights Reserved.

AND I HATE "CUTE"
JIM DAVIS

DON'T KNOCK IT, JACK. I MAKE A KILLING POSING FOR GREETING CARDS

OKAY, NERMAL. THERE'S A DOG. ...**KILL!**
9-5
© 1979 PAWS, INC. All Rights Reserved.

OH, NERMAL. NERMAL, NERMAL, NERMAL
JIM DAVIS

CRUD!
GARFIELD
9-6
© 1979 PAWS, INC. All Rights Reserved.

NERMAL SHED ALL OVER MY FOOD
GARFIELD

I CAN'T STAND CAT HAIRS UNLESS THEY'RE MY OWN
GARFIELD
JIM DAVIS

TAKE THOSE ROLLER SKATES OFF, GARFIELD. YOU LOOK RIDICULOUS
© 1979 PAWS, INC. All Rights Reserved.
9-7

JIM DAVIS

NERMAL'S LEAVING NOW. WAVE BYE-BYE, GARFIELD
9-8

I KIND OF LIKED THE LITTLE FELLER

THE WAY I LIKE INTESTINAL FLU
JIM DAVIS
© 1979 PAWS, INC. All Rights Reserved.

GARFIELD®

SPLOOSH!

OH-NO! A VICIOUS UNDERTOW IS DRAGGING ME OUT TO SEA!

I'M TOO YOUNG TO GO!
9-9

I CAN SEE THE HEADLINES NOW... "WORLD FAMOUS CAT LOST AT SEA. MILLIONS OF BEAUTIFUL GIRL CATS GRIEF-STRICKEN!"

I CAN'T MAKE IT! I'M GOING DOWN FOR THE THIRD TIME!
© 1979 PAWS, INC. All Rights Reserved.

I'D SAVE YOU, GARFIELD. BUT I'M NOT ABOUT TO GIVE A CAT MOUTH-TO-MOUTH RESUSCITATION
JIM DAVIS

9-10
YAWN
© 1979 PAWS, INC. All Rights Reserved.

OH, THIS LOOKS LIKE A NICE PLACE TO SLEEP

IF YOU DON'T MIND, GARFIELD..
JIM DAVIS

SACK! PILLAGE! MAIM! DESTROY!
9-11

BONK!

WHIMPER, LIMP, CRY, HURT, MOAN
JIM DAVIS
© 1979 PAWS, INC. All Rights Reserved.

IT'S TIME TO PUT YOUR LEASH ON FOR A NICE WALK
9-12

OH COME ON, GARFIELD. IT'S NOT THAT BAD

© 1979 PAWS, INC. All Rights Reserved.
JIM DAVIS

I KNOW YOU DON'T LIKE YOUR LEASH, GARFIELD, BUT PEOPLE ARE STARING

SO CUT THAT OUT

JIM DAVIS
© 1979 PAWS, INC. All Rights Reserved.
9-13

ODIE, YOU KNOW BETTER THAN THAT
© 1979 PAWS, INC. All Rights Reserved.

DO YOU KNOW WHAT I APPRECIATE ABOUT YOU MOST, GARFIELD ?
9-14

I'M HOUSEBROKEN
YOU'RE HOUSEBROKEN
JIM DAVIS

SOME PEOPLE SAY PETS ARE NOT CLEAN
© 1979 PAWS, INC. All Rights Reserved.
9-15

THAT MAY BE SO

BUT TRY EATING YOUR NEXT MEAL WITHOUT YOUR HANDS AND SEE HOW WELL **YOU** FARE
JIM DAVIS

SMACK
MUNCH
SLURP

ATTENTION AMERICA! I AM HEREBY DECLARING THIS WEEK **NATIONAL FAT WEEK**
© 1979 PAWS, INC. All Rights Reserved.

THIS IS THE WEEK FOR ALL YOU FAT PEOPLE TO COME OUT OF THE CLOSET
9-17

THOSE OF YOU WHO COULD GET INTO ONE, THAT IS
JIM DAVIS

THIS IS NATIONAL FAT WEEK. I WANT TO HEAR ALL YOU FAT PEOPLE SAY, "I'M FAT, AND I'M PROUD OF IT!"
© 1979 PAWS, INC. All Rights Reserved.
JIM DAVIS

LOUDER! "I'M FAT, AND I'M PROUD OF IT!"
9-18

YOU...THE PUDGY ONE IN SEATTLE, I DIDN'T HEAR YOU

HERE'S A NATIONAL FAT WEEK HANDY FAT TIP
© 1979 PAWS, INC. All Rights Reserved.

"DON'T EXERCISE." YOU'LL BE HAPPIER

HAVE YOU EVER SEEN A JOGGER LAUGH?
9-19
JIM DAVIS

HERE'S A NATIONAL FAT WEEK SKINNY JOKE
9-20
JIM DAVIS

HOW MANY SKINNY PEOPLE DOES IT TAKE TO FILL A SHOWER?

I DON'T KNOW. THEY KEEP SLIPPING DOWN THE DRAIN
© 1979 PAWS, INC. All Rights Reserved.

HERE'S THE NATIONAL FAT WEEK "WEIGHT-HEIGHT CHART"
© 1979 PAWS, INC. All Rights Reserved.

ACCORDING TO THIS, IF YOU WEIGH 200 POUNDS, YOU SHOULD BE 6'4"
9-21

THAT MEANS IF YOU'RE UNDER 6'4" YOU'RE NOT OVERWEIGHT, YOU'RE UNDERTALL
JIM DAVIS

WELL, FAT BROTHERS AND SISTERS, THIS IS THE LAST DAY OF NATIONAL FAT WEEK
9-22

JUST REMEMBER, "ROUND IS BEAUTIFUL"

NOW GET OUT THERE AND EAT A CHICKEN FRANCHISE
JIM DAVIS
© 1979 PAWS, INC. All Rights Reserved.

CARTOONIST'S NOTE:
TODAY'S GARFIELD STRIP IS TO BE READ ONLY BY FAT PEOPLE, OR PEOPLE WITH FAT TENDENCIES. YOU SKINNY ONES CAN READ THE OTHER STRIPS, OR JOG, OR DRINK A GLASS OF WATER, OR WHATEVER IT IS SKINNY PEOPLE DO. ...I WOULDN'T KNOW.

BE CAREFUL THERE, GARFIELD

HANGING ON THE DRAPES CAN BE VERY PAINFUL
© 1979 PAWS, INC. All Rights Reserved.

'CAUSE I'M GONNA BREAK YOUR LEGS IF YOU DON'T GET OFF THEM THIS INSTANT!
JIM DAVIS
9-24

GASP! CHOKE! WHEEZE!
9-25

OH NO YOU DON'T, GARFIELD

SO MUCH FOR THE OLD "PLAY-SICK-AND-GRAB-THE-CHICKEN-WHEN-YOUR-OWNER-CALLS-THE-VET" ROUTINE
JIM DAVIS
© 1979 PAWS, INC. All Rights Reserved.

GARFIELD! BREAKFAST!
9-26

BONK!

I DID IT AGAIN. I GOT UP BEFORE I WOKE UP
© 1979 PAWS, INC. All Rights Reserved.
JIM DAVIS

WAG
WAG
WAG
© 1979 PAWS, INC. All Rights Reserved.

STOMP!

WAG
WAG
WAG
9-27
JIM DAVIS

© 1979 PAWS, INC. All Rights Reserved.
9-28

MEYOW

LET ME GUESS. YOU WERE IN THE PICKLED HERRING AGAIN
JIM DAVIS

EAT UP, GARFIELD
MEYOW
GARFIELD
© 1979 PAWS, INC. All Rights Reserved.
9-29

IT SAYS HERE THIS IS A "NEW IMPROVED" CAT FOOD
MUNCH
MUNCH
GARFIELD

MEYOW!
GARFIELD
JIM DAVIS

GARFIELD®

9-30

OH, DARN

JON'S FLOWER GARDEN GOT A LITTLE OVER-FROLICKED
JIM DAVIS
© 1979 PAWS, INC. All Rights Reserved.

WE'RE GOING TO SEE YOUR VETERINARIAN TODAY, GARFIELD
10-1

SHE'S ONE CUTE CHICKY-BOO. I'D MARRY HER IN A SECOND
© 1979 PAWS, INC. All Rights Reserved.

IT'S COMFORTING TO KNOW THE HIGH VALUES PLACED ON THE SACRED INSTI-TUTION OF MARRIAGE ARE STILL WITH US TODAY
IN A HALF-SECOND!
JIM DAVIS

© 1979 PAWS, INC. All Rights Reserved.

THAT LIZ IS SURE A GREAT LOOKING HUNK OF VETERINARIAN

SHE HAS THE ONE QUALITY I DESIRE MOST IN A WOMAN
SHE'S BREATHING
10-2
JIM DAVIS

BE RIGHT WITH YOU, MR. ARBUCKLE
© 1979 PAWS, INC. All Rights Reserved.

I'LL BE HERE WITH BELLS ON, DOCTOR
THAT MAKES FOR AN INTERESTING MENTAL PICTURE

WHY DOES SHE ALWAYS PUT ME DOWN?
YOU'RE SO PUTDOWNABLE
10-3
JIM DAVIS

HOW ABOUT GOING OUT WITH ME, DOCTOR?
I WOULDN'T GO OUT WITH YOU IF YOU WERE THE LAST MAN ON EARTH
10-4

THEN HOW ABOUT SOMETIME AFTER THAT?
THAT'S A GOOD ONE
JIM DAVIS
© 1979 PAWS, INC. All Rights Reserved.

WHY WON'T YOU GO OUT WITH ME, DOCTOR?
BECAUSE I HATE YOUR GUTS
10-5

DOES THIS MEAN MARRIAGE IS OUT OF THE QUESTION?
DON QUIXOTE STRIKES AGAIN
JIM DAVIS
© 1979 PAWS, INC. All Rights Reserved.

HOW ABOUT A DATE, DOC?
NO WAY
10-6

MMMM

GREAT! SEE YOU AT EIGHT
IF YOU CAN'T CONVINCE'M, CONFUSE'M
JIM DAVIS
© 1979 PAWS, INC. All Rights Reserved.

GARFIELD®

CAUTION

HMMM, WET CEMENT

SPLUT!
OOPS!

© 1979 PAWS, INC. All Rights Reserved.

BARK! BARK!

SLURP

LASSIE WOULD HAVE GONE FOR HELP
JIM DAVIS
10-7

I SUPPOSE YOU WANT TO KNOW HOW MY DATE WENT WITH LIZ, THE VET...WELL DON'T ASK
I WON'T
10-8

SHE DIDN'T SHOW. OLD JON GOT STOOD UP
I DON'T WANT TO HEAR ABOUT IT

YOU KNOW, GARFIELD. I LIKE YOU BETTER THAN PEOPLE
TELL ME MORE
© 1979 PAWS, INC. All Rights Reserved.
JIM DAVIS

MUNCH MUNCH MUNCH
10-9

SMACK! SLURP! GOBBLE!

© 1979 PAWS, INC. All Rights Reserved.
JIM DAVIS

MY AUNT EVELYN IS THE NEATEST CAT I KNOW
© 1979 PAWS, INC. All Rights Reserved.
10-10

SHE PLUCKED ALL THE HAIR OFF HER BODY SO SHE WOULDN'T SHED ON THE FURNITURE

NOW SHE'S LIVING WITH A FAMILY IN L.A. THAT THINKS SHE'S A CHIHUAHUA
JIM DAVIS

YIP!
YIP!
YIP!
© 1979 PAWS, INC. All Rights Reserved.

YIP!
YIP!
YIP!

FOR THE LAST TIME, ODIE, **YOU** CHASE THE **TAIL**
JIM DAVIS
10-11

GARFIELD, MUST YOU DO EVERYTHING I DO?
10-12

THAT WASN'T VERY NICE

AFTER ALL, CATS ARE JUST LITTLE PEOPLE WITH FUR AND FANGS
JIM DAVIS
© 1979 PAWS, INC. All Rights Reserved.

© 1979 PAWS, INC. All Rights Reserved.
10-13

FWIP
FWIP
FWIP
FWIP
FWIP
FWIP
SHOOP!

A VENETIAN TONGUE
JIM DAVIS

GARFIELD®

WAKE UP, SLEEPYHEAD!

WE'RE HAVING BREAKFAST ON THE PATIO THIS MORNING

BECAUSE I WANT TO SHARE THIS BEAUTIFUL SUNRISE WITH YOU
10-14
JIM DAVIS

WHERE ELSE CAN YOU FIND A LIVING, BREATHING WORK OF ART CREATED JUST FOR YOU? FRESH WITH THE PROMISE OF A BRIGHT NEW DAY

HAVE YOU EVER SEEN A MORE GLORIOUS SIGHT, GARFIELD?.. UH, GARFIELD?
© 1979 PAWS, INC. All Rights Reserved.

GET YOUR FACE OUT OF THE SCRAMBLED EGGS, GARFIELD
ZZZZ

BATH TIME, GARFIELD
10-15

SQUIP!
© 1979 PAWS, INC. All Rights Reserved.

LARD
JIM DAVIS

GOTCHA!
10-16

BATH TIME!
SPLOOSH!

NOW WHERE COULD POOKY BE?
JIM DAVIS
© 1979 PAWS, INC. All Rights Reserved.

SOAP
© 1979 PAWS, INC. All Rights Reserved.
10-17

SOAP

CATS!
SOAP
JIM DAVIS

10-18

ZIP!!

© 1979 PAWS, INC. All Rights Reserved.
FOUL! FOUL! NO FAIR! FOUL!
SOAP
JIM DAVIS

MORNIN'
GOOD MORNING, IRMA
10-19

THE COFFEE'S STRONG, HON. YOU'D BETTER GET IT BEFORE IT GETS YOU
IS IT HOT?
© 1979 PAWS, INC. All Rights Reserved.

YUP
THIS ISN'T ONE OF YOUR BETTER DINERS
JIM DAVIS

MY, YOU LOOK NICE TODAY, IRMA
ARE YOU KIDDING?
10-20

WHEN I COME TO WORK I WEAR BASE AND LIPSTICK AND THAT'S IT, HON. I DON'T PUT ON EYES UNLESS I HAVE A HOT DATE. YOU KNOW WHAT I MEAN?

© 1979 PAWS, INC. All Rights Reserved.

I DIDN'T EVEN SHAVE MY LEGS
THIS DEFINITELY ISN'T ONE OF YOUR BETTER DINERS
JIM DAVIS

GARFIELD®

BOY, AM I BORED
© 1979 PAWS, INC. All Rights Reserved.

BORED, BORED, BORED, BORED
10-21
JIM DAVIS

ARGHHH!

I FEEL BETTER ALREADY

© 1979 PAWS, INC. All Rights Reserved.

SMACK!
10-22

I HATE PATIO DOORS
JIM DAVIS

10-23
© 1979 PAWS, INC. All Rights Reserved.

HEY, GARFIELD, WHERE'S ODIE?
HE'S EASY ENOUGH TO FIND

JIM DAVIS
JUST FOLLOW THE SLOBBER

CAT FOOD
GARFIELD
10-24
© 1979 PAWS, INC. All Rights Reserved.

Ingredient: gunk
CAT FOOD
GARFIELD

I SUSPECTED AS MUCH
GARFIELD
JIM DAVIS

FOR THE LAST TIME, NO, GARFIELD
GARFIELD
10-25

WHAT'S THE PROBLEM?
© 1979 PAWS, INC. All Rights Reserved.

HE WANTS TO SEE A WINE LIST
JIM DAVIS

YOU MAY HAVE THE LEFTOVERS WHEN I'M THROUGH, GARFIELD
© 1979 PAWS, INC. All Rights Reserved.

KONG!

YOU DON'T HAVE TO BE PATIENT WHEN YOU'RE AS BIG AS I AM
10-26
JIM DAVIS

ARE YOU STILL HAVING BREAKFAST ?
GARFIELD
10-27
© 1979 PAWS, INC. All Rights Reserved.

YOU'VE SPENT AN HOUR EATING YOUR CEREAL
GARFIELD

YOU KNOW I DON'T LIKE RAISINS
GARFIELD
JIM DAVIS

GARFIELD®

SLIT!
10-28

MUNCH
SMACK
SLURP

PTOOEY!

BURP

GARFIELD WENT TO SO MUCH TROUBLE I HATED TO SPOIL IT FOR HIM
JIM DAVIS

GOOD BOY, GARFIELD. GIVE ME THE PAPER
© 1979 PAWS, INC. All Rights Reserved.
10-29

EITHER I GET BREAKFAST OR YOU'LL NEVER SEE THIS PAPER ALIVE AGAIN

WHY IS THERE ALWAYS A STRING ATTACHED?!
NOTHING'S FREE, PAL
JIM DAVIS

© 1979 PAWS, INC. All Rights Reserved.

FLIP!

JIM DAVIS
I CAN TAKE A HINT
10-30

I HAVE SOME-THING FOR THAT APPETITE OF YOURS, GARFIELD
© 1979 PAWS, INC. All Rights Reserved.

CLOSE YOUR EYES AND OPEN YOUR MOUTH

JIM DAVIS
10-31

HERE'S A HANDY HINT FOR YOU BACHELORS OUT THERE
© 1979 PAWS, INC. All Rights Reserved.

YOU CAN KEEP YOUR LAUNDRY DETERGENT DRY

BY SEALING IT IN A COOKIE JAR
11-1
JIM DAVIS

LET'S GO SEE THE VET, GARFIELD

© 1979 PAWS, INC. All Rights Reserved.

I HAVE A TEN O'CLOCK APPOINTMENT
11-2
JIM DAVIS

VETERINARY CLINIC
© 1979 PAWS, INC. All Rights Reserved.

HERE, PETEY. HERE, PETEY. WHERE ARE YOU?

11-3
VETERINARY CLINIC
BURP!
JIM DAVIS

GARFIELD®

MUNCH
MUNCH
MUNCH
GARFIELD

WHEW! I COULDN'T EAT ANOTHER BITE
GARFIELD

GARFIELD

RRRR
GARFIELD
11-4

ROWR
GARFIELD
© 1979 PAWS, INC. All Rights Reserved.

RRR
GARFIELD

GARFIELD

GARFIELD
JIM DAVIS

PACK YOUR BAGS, GARFIELD. WE'RE GOING ON VACATION
© 1979 PAWS, INC. All Rights Reserved.
11-5

GOOD IDEA

I COULD USE THE REST
JIM DAVIS

WE HAVE A LONG WAY TO GO, GARFIELD
JIM DAVIS

I WISH YOU ENJOYED RIDING IN A CAR MORE
© 1979 PAWS, INC. All Rights Reserved.

YOU'RE TOO TENSE
11-6

I'D LIKE A ROOM FOR THE NIGHT
11-7

ANY PETS?
NOPE
© 1979 PAWS, INC. All Rights Reserved.

JIM DAVIS

© 1979 PAWS, INC. All Rights Reserved.
JIM DAVIS

LOOK AT THAT, GARFIELD. WHAT DO YOU...
11-8

...UH, THINK

WHEN I THINK OF SAND, I THINK OF SUN, SURF AND GETTING A GOOD TAN

WHAT DO YOU THINK OF WHEN YOU THINK OF SAND, GARFIELD?
11-9
© 1979 PAWS, INC. All Rights Reserved.

ON SECOND THOUGHT, SCRATCH THAT QUESTION
JIM DAVIS

11-10
FRED'S FRESH FISH
© 1979 PAWS, INC. All Rights Reserved.

FRED'S FRESH FISH

JIM DAVIS

GARFIELD®

POKE!

GRRRRRR

CHOKE!
GASP!
11-11

KICK!

KONG!
JIM DAVIS
© 1979 PAWS, INC. All Rights Reserved.

rain (rān) n. 1. water falling to earth in drops

11/12
2. a mild depressant
JIM DAVIS
© 1979 PAWS, INC. All Rights Reserved.

© 1979 PAWS, INC. All Rights Reserved.
ZZZZ

SCREECH!

CHASING CARS AGAIN, GARFIELD?
JIM DAVIS
11-13

WHY ARE WE PLACED ON THIS EARTH? WHAT IS OUR PURPOSE? WHAT IS OUR MISSION IN LIFE?
© 1979 PAWS, INC. All Rights Reserved.

THANK YOU SO MUCH FOR YOUR PROMPT REPLY
11-14
JIM DAVIS

11-15
© 1979 PAWS, INC. All Rights Reserved.

JIM DAVIS
NICE TRY, HOT SHOT

HOW'S YOUR COFFEE, HON?
IT'S A BIT STRONG

SAY IT'S NOT SO! SAY IT'S NOT SO! I COULD JUST SHOOT MYSELF!
11-16

YOU USUALLY DON'T FIND ONE THAT DEDICATED
IT'S HER LIFE
© 1979 PAWS, INC. All Rights Reserved.
JIM DAVIS

11-17
I HATE IT WHEN GARFIELD FALLS ASLEEP IN MY LAP
ZZZ

HE SNUGGLES UP
ZZZ

AND DIGS IN
ZZZ
© 1979 PAWS, INC. All Rights Reserved.
JIM DAVIS

GARFIELD®

BOING!
BOING!
JIM DAVIS
© 1979 PAWS, INC. All Rights Reserved.

MUNCH
MUNCH
MUNCH
GARFIELD

CLOBBER!
GARFIELD

LOVE IS A
FICKLE THING
GARFIELD
11-18

AH-AH-AH
JIM DAVIS

AHCHOO!
© 1979 PAWS, INC. All Rights Reserved.

SNIFF
11-19

SCRATCH THE SOFA ALL YOU LIKE, GARFIELD

REVERSE PSYCHOLOGY
JIM DAVIS

© 1979 PAWS, INC. All Rights Reserved.
REVERSE REVERSE PSYCHOLOGY
11-20

IT'S TIME YOU STARTED TAKING VITAMINS, GARFIELD
NO WAY, PAL. MY BODY'S A TEMPLE
© 1979 PAWS, INC. All Rights Reserved.
11-21

I PUT THEM IN THIS LASAGNA

EVEN A TEMPLE NEEDS HIS VITAMIN C
JIM DAVIS

DOESN'T IT BOTHER YOU THAT YOUR CAT IS ALWAYS UNDERFOOT?

NOT AT ALL. GARFIELD IS VERY FOND OF ME
© 1979 PAWS, INC. All Rights Reserved.

11·22
WE'RE INSEPARABLE, AREN'T WE, GARFIELD?
YOU'RE STANDING ON MY TAIL
JIM DAVIS

I OFTEN WONDER WHAT GOES ON IN THAT COMPLEX MIND OF YOURS, GARFIELD
BZZZZZZZZZZZZZ

WOULDN'T IT BE WONDERFUL IF HUMANS AND ANIMALS COULD COMMUNICATE?
SMACK!
JIM DAVIS
© 1979 PAWS, INC. All Rights Reserved.

WHAT WOULD YOU SAY TO ME IF YOU COULD TALK RIGHT NOW?
I JUST KILLED A FLY SOMEWHERE ON YOUR RAISIN TOAST
11-23

THAT'S A NASTY COLD YOU HAVE THERE, GARFIELD
SNIFF
© 1979 PAWS, INC. All Rights Reserved.

WE'LL TAKE YOU TO THE VET AND GET YOU FIXED RIGHT UP
JIM DAVIS

NEVER SAY "FIXED" TO AN ANIMAL PERSON
11-24

GARFIELD®

THERE'S NOTHING LIKE A BRISK MORNING JOG IN THERMAL UNDERWEAR

HMMM. A THREAD

© 1979 PAWS, INC. All Rights Reserved.
11-25
JIM DAVIS

SLAM

VERY FUNNY, GARFIELD

GET OFF THE CEILING, GARFIELD
JIM DAVIS

GET OUT OF THE GLOVE COMPARTMENT, GARFIELD
© 1979 PAWS, INC. All Rights Reserved.

GET BACK IN THE GLOVE COMPARTMENT, GARFIELD
11·26

JIM DAVIS

© 1979 PAWS, INC. All Rights Reserved.

GET YOUR FACE OFF THE WINDSHIELD, GARFIELD
11·27

WHAT IS IT, GARFIELD? WHAT ARE YOU TRYING TO TELL ME ?
11·28

OH
© 1979 PAWS, INC. All Rights Reserved.

YOU'RE CARSICK, YOU SAY
JIM DAVIS

JIM DAVIS

© 1979 PAWS, INC. All Rights Reserved.

STOP PLAYING WITH THE POWER SEAT, GARFIELD
11-29

DINNER'S ON, GARFIELD. WE HAVE LASAGNA AND CHICKEN AND MASHED POTATOES
JIM DAVIS
11-30

LET'S SEE, I THINK I'LL HAVE . . .
© 1979 PAWS, INC. All Rights Reserved.

A PEANUT BUTTER AND JELLY SANDWICH

WELL, GARFIELD, THAT'S THE LAST TIME THE HAMILTONS EVER ASK US OVER
© 1979 PAWS, INC. All Rights Reserved.
JIM DAVIS

I HOPE YOU LEARNED A LESSON FROM THIS EVENING
I SURE DID

NEVER SHARPEN YOUR CLAWS ON A WATER BED
12-1

GARFIELD®

HAVE YOU EVER NOTICED HOW MUCH SOME PEOPLE LOOK LIKE THEIR PETS, GARFIELD?
© 1979 PAWS, INC. All Rights Reserved.

HEE HEE
HEE

HA-HA HA
HA

12-2

JIM DAVIS

GUESS WHO'S COME TO VISIT US THIS WEEK, GARFIELD?
12-3

NERMAL! THE WORLD'S CUTEST KITTEN

YOU'RE TESTING ME, AREN'T YOU?!
© 1979 PAWS, INC. All Rights Reserved.
JIM DAVIS

HOW CUTE!
JIM DAVIS

© 1979 PAWS, INC. All Rights Reserved.

12-4

HOW CUTE!
HOP
HOP
HOP
© 1979 PAWS, INC. All Rights Reserved.

BOOM!
BOOM!
BOOM!

SOMEHOW, GARFIELD, YOUR GRASP OF "CUTE" IS A LITTLE SHAKY
12-5
JIM DAVIS

SCRATCH!
SCRATCH!
SCRATCH!
SCRATCH!
© 1979 PAWS, INC. All Rights Reserved.
JIM DAVIS

THERE'S ONE NICE THING ABOUT HAVING ANOTHER CAT AROUND THE HOUSE
12-6

NERMAL!

I'M TIRED OF COMPETING WITH THAT NERMAL. I THINK I'LL GIVE HIM A GOOD POUNDING TODAY
© 1979 PAWS, INC. All Rights Reserved.

WHERE IS THAT LITTLE FUZZBALL? HE COULD BE ANYWHERE
GARFIELD

GARFIELD
12-7
JIM DAVIS

IT'S TIME WE DETERMINED WHO'S MASTER OF THIS HOUSEHOLD
12-8
© 1979 PAWS, INC. All Rights Reserved.

SMACK!

HOW DID HE DO THAT?
JIM DAVIS

GARFIELD®

© 1979 PAWS, INC. All Rights Reserved.

JIM DAVIS

WOULD YOU LIKE TO COME IN, GARFIELD ?
12-9

© 1979 PAWS, INC. All Rights Reserved.

JIM DAVIS

IT'S TIME WE TALKED ABOUT THIS COFFEE DEPENDENCY OF YOURS, GARFIELD
AHHH
12-10

PLIP!
© 1979 PAWS, INC. All Rights Reserved.

HOT! HOT! HOT! HOT!

JIM DAVIS
12-11

© 1979 PAWS, INC. All Rights Reserved.
JIM DAVIS

GET OFF THE PIANO, ODIE. YOU'RE MAKING TOO MUCH RACKET

12-12
AND YOU...

GARFIELD! THAT'S BEAUTIFUL!

WE'LL GO ON THE ROAD. WE'LL MAKE A MILLION! WE'RE RICH!

© 1979 PAWS, INC. All Rights Reserved.
JIM DAVIS
12-13

CLICK!
STOP PLAYING WITH THE FLASHLIGHT, GARFIELD
© 1979 PAWS, INC. All Rights Reserved.
12-14
JIM DAVIS

JIM DAVIS
YOUR PICTURE 4 FOR 50¢
© 1979 PAWS, INC. All Rights Reserved.
12-15

GARFIELD®

LET'S GO LOOK AT NEW FURNITURE, GARFIELD

FURNITURE CITY
GEE, THIS SOFA'S NICE. WHAT DO YOU THINK, GARFIELD?

© 1979 PAWS, INC. All Rights Reserved.
GARFIELD?

POW!

KOOOOSH
POP!
POP!
SSSSSS
POW!
PLIF
12-16

CONGRATULATIONS, SIR. YOU ARE NOW THE PROUD OWNER OF 23 SLIGHTLY CLAWED INFLATABLE CHAIRS
I HAVEN'T HAD SO MUCH FUN SINCE GRANNY GOT HER TAIL CAUGHT IN THE WRINGER
JIM DAVIS

BAT-
BAT-
JIM DAVIS

ZIP!
12-17
© 1979 PAWS, INC. All Rights Reserved.

I'LL LAY YOU TEN TO ONE I'M HERE TILL SATURDAY

WHAT A BUMMER. HERE I AM WRAPPED UP IN A WINDOW BLIND

JUST A BUMP IN THE ROAD OF DESTINY, JUST A HUMP ON THE CAMEL OF FATE, JUST A LUMP IN THE THROAT OF MISFORTUNE

HEY! YOU **DO** HAVE TO SUFFER TO WRITE!
JIM DAVIS
12-18
© 1979 PAWS, INC. All Rights Reserved.

IF I EXPAND THE MUSCLES IN MY BODY, MAYBE I CAN BURST MY WAY OUT OF THIS BLIND

DRAT! I FORGOT
12-19

WHAT MUSCLES?
JIM DAVIS
© 1979 PAWS, INC. All Rights Reserved.

12-20

JIM DAVIS
© 1979 PAWS, INC. All Rights Reserved.
I WAS AFRAID OF THAT

12-21
JIM DAVIS
HEY, GARFIELD

WHAT ARE YOU DOING UP THERE?

IN A WORLD FULL OF IDIOTS, I GET THE GRAND HIGH LLAMA
© 1979 PAWS, INC. All Rights Reserved.

JIM DAVIS
© 1979 PAWS, INC. All Rights Reserved.
LET ME GET YOU OUT OF THAT BLIND, GARFIELD

12-22

GARFIELD®

© 1979 PAWS, INC. All Rights Reserved.
JIM DAVIS

UH-OH! HERE COMES JON!

THE PERFECT CRIME

OH, GARFIELD

HAVE YOU, PERCHANCE, SEEN MY CHICKEN?
12-23

JUST ONE BITE OF CHICKEN AND THAT'S IT, GARFIELD

12-24
© 1979 PAWS, INC. All Rights Reserved.

IF YOU SWALLOW, I'LL TIE A KNOT IN YOUR NECK
JIM DAVIS

WHATEVER YOUR BELIEFS, THE CHRISTMAS SEASON REPRESENTS PEACE, LOVE AND CHARITY AMONG PEOPLE EVERYWHERE
12-25

MERRY CHRISTMAS AND SEASON'S GREETINGS

SOMETIMES I'M SO SENTIMENTAL I COULD JUST KISS MYSELF
JIM DAVIS
© 1979 PAWS, INC. All Rights Reserved.

I FROZE A SPECIAL TREAT FOR YOU, GARFIELD

OH, GOODY
12-26

CAT FOOD ON A STICK
JIM DAVIS
© 1979 PAWS, INC. All Rights Reserved.

IT'S TRUE CATS ALWAYS LAND ON THEIR FEET

12-27

THE THINGS I DO FOR THIS STRIP
© 1979 PAWS, INC. All Rights Reserved.
JIM DAVIS

© 1979 PAWS, INC. All Rights Reserved.
12-28

SPIDERS ARE CURIOUS INSECTS TO SEE. THEIR WEBS ARE REALLY NEAT.

BUT HOW DO THEY WEAVE THEM ELABORATELY, WHEN ALL THEY HAVE IS FEET?
JIM DAVIS

GARFIELD AND I CAN ACTUALLY COMMUNICATE. WATCH THIS...

WOULD YOU LIKE TO TAKE A BATH, GARFIELD?
12-29

GARFIELD SAID "NO"
© 1979 PAWS, INC. All Rights Reserved.
JIM DAVIS

GARFIELD®

CRASH!

GARFIELD! YOU BROKE MY FERN!!

I RAISED THAT FERN FROM A FROND!
12·30

WHAT DID THAT FERN EVER DO TO YOU ?!!

WHY, I HAVE A NOTION TO... UH ... TO

I...UH
© 1979 PAWS, INC. All Rights Reserved.

YOU'RE SO CUTE
LIKE PUTTY IN MY PAWS
JIM DAVIS

THIS YEAR I RESOLVE TO LOSE WEIGHT...
12-31

TO BE NICER TO DOGS...

AND TO SPROUT WINGS AND FLY
JIM DAVIS
© 1979 PAWS, INC. All Rights Reserved.

SO THIS IS 1980
© 1980 PAWS, INC. All Rights Reserved.
1-1

FEELS ABOUT THE SAME
JIM DAVIS

YOU'RE A SWELL CAT, GARFIELD
© 1980 PAWS, INC. All Rights Reserved.
1-2

IT'S TIME WE DID MORE THINGS TOGETHER

LIKE GIVE YOU A BATH!
I KNEW IT! I KNEW IT!
JIM DAVIS

DARN THE TORPEDOES! FULL SPEED AHEAD!
1-3
© 1980 PAWS, INC. All Rights Reserved.

NEVER HAVE SO FEW GIVEN SO MUCH TO SO MANY

QUIT DAWDLING, GARFIELD
HOW DARE YOU SPEAK THAT WAY TO THE PRESIDENT OF THE UNITED STATES
JIM DAVIS

JUST AS I SUSPECTED
JIM DAVIS
1-4

THE FLOOR IS FREEZING

CLOP!
CLOP!
GARFIELD
© 1980 PAWS, INC. All Rights Reserved.

© 1980 PAWS, INC. All Rights Reserved.

1-5
JIM DAVIS

GARFIELD®

BACK OFF, GARFIELD. THAT TURKEY LEG IS FOR MY LUNCH

AHCHOO!

WIPE
WIPE
WIPE
WIPE

SCRATCH
SCRATCH
SCRATCH
SCRATCH
SCRATCH
SCRATCH
© 1980 PAWS, INC. All Rights Reserved.
1-6

WOULD YOU LIKE A TURKEY LEG, GARFIELD ?
ONLY IF YOU DON'T WANT IT
JIM DAVIS

SLURP!
© 1980 PAWS, INC. All Rights Reserved.

THE COFFEE'S TOO HOT, GARFIELD

THANKS FOR TELLING ME
JIM DAVIS
1-7

WHAT WOULD YOU LIKE FOR BREAKFAST, GARFIELD?
SOMETHING DIFFERENT!
© 1980 PAWS, INC. All Rights Reserved.
1-8

THE USUAL, YOU SAY?
NO! NO! NO! NO! NO! NO!

ONE USUAL COMING UP!
IT'S THINGS LIKE THIS THAT CONTRIBUTE TO THE HIGH SUICIDE RATE AMONG CATS
GARFIELD
JIM DAVIS

YIP!
PUNT!

© 1980 PAWS, INC. All Rights Reserved.
1-9
JIM DAVIS

THROW ME A ROLL, JON
© 1980 PAWS, INC. All Rights Reserved.

GULP!
1-10

JIM DAVIS
PASS ME A ROLL, JON

HOW MANY TIMES HAVE I TOLD YOU NOT TO BEG AT THE TABLE?

SOMETIMES ODIE IS A REAL PROBLEM
1-11
JIM DAVIS
© 1980 PAWS, INC. All Rights Reserved.

I WISH I HAD YOUR PROBLEM

OH, NO, GARFIELD. YOU'RE NOT GETTING MY CHICKEN TODAY
1-12

I KNOW ALL YOUR PLOYS, BUDDY BOY. I'M WATCHING YOU LIKE A HAWK
© 1980 PAWS, INC. All Rights Reserved.

JIM DAVIS

GARFIELD®

1-13

© 1980 PAWS, INC. All Rights Reserved.
JIM DAVIS

I THOUGHT SO

SNIFF
1-14

OH DOE! I'M CUBBING DOWN WID A CODE

LOOG, I CAN HARDLY EBBEN UNDERSTAD BY OWN THOUGHTS
JIM DAVIS
© 1980 PAWS, INC. All Rights Reserved.

SNIFF
© 1980 PAWS, INC. All Rights Reserved.
1-15

OH, ICKY POO! GARFIELD'S GOT A COLD. HE'S DISEASED! EVERYONE STAND BACK!

BERRY FUDDY
JIM DAVIS

AH-CHOO!
© 1980 PAWS, INC. All Rights Reserved.
1-16

IT'S YOURS, GARFIELD

THIS COULD BE THE START OF SOMETHING GRAND
JIM DAVIS

I HATE CODES
SNIFF
© 1980 PAWS, INC. All Rights Reserved.
1-17

I CAN'T BELEEB HOW MUCH MY HEAD IS STUFFED UBB

JIM DAVIS

SNIFF
© 1980 PAWS, INC. All Rights Reserved.
1-18

ARRRGH!!!

COLDS CAN BE FRUSTRATING CAN'T THEY, OL' BUDDY?
JIM DAVIS

YOUR COUGH SOUNDS BETTER, GARFIELD
HACK HACK
© 1980 PAWS, INC. All Rights Reserved.

IT SHOULD
1-19

I'VE BEEN PRACTICING ALL NIGHT
JIM DAVIS

GARFIELD®

MY CHICKEN!!!

AS LONG AS YOU ATE MY CHICKEN, GARFIELD, WHY DON'T YOU...

EAT MY MASHED POTATOES!
© 1980 PAWS, INC. All Rights Reserved.
1-20

AND MY PEAS!

AND MY RADISHES! AND MY CELERY!

I THINK JON'S UPSET
JIM DAVIS

I LOVE A CHEERY FIRE IN A FIREPLACE
© 1980 PAWS, INC. All Rights Reserved.
1-21

FOOMP!

IT'S THE SPARKS I'M NOT TOO FOND OF
JIM DAVIS

GARFIELD! LUNCH TIME!
1-22

I HATE IT WHEN MY FEET GO TO SLEEP
JIM DAVIS
© 1980 PAWS, INC. All Rights Reserved.

FRANK, MEET GARFIELD
HI, GARFIELD
JIM DAVIS
1-23

ROWRRRR!

SOME PEOPLE RUB ME THE WRONG WAY
© 1980 PAWS, INC. All Rights Reserved.

LET'S TALK ABOUT DOGS... WHAT ARE DOGS ?
© 1980 PAWS, INC. All Rights Reserved.

1-24

ARE THEY VEGETABLE OR MINERAL ?
JIM DAVIS

GARÇON, I'LL HAVE THE ESCARGÓT AND TRUFFLES FOR AN APPETIZER, THEN THE DUCK À L'ORANGE FLAMBÉ AND SOME CAPPUCCINO
JIM DAVIS
© 1980 PAWS, INC. All Rights Reserved.

EAT UP, PAL
GARFIELD

TALK ABOUT LOWERING ONE'S SIGHTS...
GARFIELD
1-25

HERE'S YOUR COFFEE, HON

CRASH!
1-26

THIS ROLLER SKATING CRAZE IS GETTING OUT OF HAND
© 1980 PAWS, INC. All Rights Reserved.
JIM DAVIS

GARFIELD®

LET'S TIGHTEN THAT LEASH, GARFIELD
I HATE LEASHES

FFT!
ROWR!

DON'T WORRY, GARFIELD. SOME KIND PASSER-BY WILL UNTIE US
1-27

UH, SIR? PARDON ME MA'AM... HEY YOU THERE... UH...

SLAM
HI, JON
HI, LYMAN

WHAT TOOK YOU SO LONG?

I HAD TO DRAG MYSELF HOME WITH MY LIPS
© 1980 PAWS, INC. All Rights Reserved.
JIM DAVIS

MORNING, LIZ. JON HERE. I'M BRINGING GARFIELD IN FOR A CHECKUP TODAY
© 1980 PAWS, INC. All Rights Reserved.

I KNOW YOU'VE BEEN WANTING TO GET TO KNOW ME BETTER, SO WHY DON'T YOU MAKE IT A LATE APPOINTMENT AND WE'LL GO TO DINNER AFTERWARD
1-28

JON... JON ARBUCKLE
JIM DAVIS

HI, DOCTOR! REMEMBER ME? JON? YOUR KNIGHT IN SHINING ARMOR?
© 1980 PAWS, INC. All Rights Reserved.
1-29

OH YES, I REMEMBER

NAMES ESCAPE ME, BUT I NEVER FORGET A TWIT
JIM DAVIS

IN ORDER TO BECOME A VETERINARIAN, YOU MUST HAVE TO HAVE A GOOD MIND FOR A WOMAN
1-30

I HAVE A GOOD MIND FOR A MAN
© 1980 PAWS, INC. All Rights Reserved.

YOU ALSO HAVE A GREAT BODY FOR A MAN
JIM DAVIS

1-31
HOW ABOUT A DATE, LIZ?
© 1980 PAWS, INC. All Rights Reserved.

COULD YOU MAKE IT THROUGH THE NIGHT IF I SAID NO?
YES

NO
WHEN IT COMES TO SLOW WITS, JON IS A GENIUS
JIM DAVIS

SAY, "AH," GARFIELD
2-1

I'LL TAKE YOUR TEMPERATURE IF YOU DON'T SAY, "AH"

AH
JIM DAVIS
© 1980 PAWS, INC. All Rights Reserved.

I KNOW YOU'RE JUST A VETERINARIAN, LIZ, BUT I'VE HAD THESE DIZZY SPELLS LATELY...
2-2

WELL NOW, WHY DON'T WE JUST CHECK YOUR BLOOD PRESSURE

UH... DOCTOR
JIM DAVIS
© 1980 PAWS, INC. All Rights Reserved.

GARFIELD®

OH BOY, IS IT CHILLY THIS MORNING

SPLASH
SPLASH
SPLASH

SIP

GARGLE
GARGLE
GARGLE

GULP

THAT FEELS SO WARM

AHHH
JPM DAVIS

YOU REALLY ENJOY YOUR COFFEE, DON'T YOU, GARFIELD?
2-3

READY FOR TENNIS?
AS SOON AS I FEED GARFIELD. HE'S HUNGRY
JIM DAVIS

HOW DO YOU KNOW THAT?
2-4

I HAVE MY WAYS
© 1980 PAWS, INC. All Rights Reserved.

HERE'S A PICTURE OF GARFIELD AT THE ZOO
© 1980 PAWS, INC. All Rights Reserved
2-5

HERE'S GARFIELD SITTING NEXT TO A VERY RARE $ 300 PARROT

HERE'S A PICTURE OF ME SHELLING OUT 300 BUCKS FOR GARFIELD'S LUNCH
JIM DAVIS

HELP YOURSELF, GARFIELD
2-6

WOULD YOU LIKE A LITTLE COFFEE IN THAT SUGAR?
JIM DAVIS
© 1980 PAWS, INC. All Rights Reserved.

THIS SHOULD BLOW JON'S MIND. ME, GARFIELD, BEING NICE TO ODIE
PAT PAT
2-7

HEH HEH, HOW NICE
PAT PAT

THAT WAS A JOKE, YOU TWIT
JIM DAVIS
© 1980 PAWS, INC. All Rights Reserved.

© 1980 PAWS, INC. All Rights Reserved.
2-8

PUSH!

THIS TABLE WASN'T BIG ENOUGH FOR THE BOTH OF US
JIM DAVIS

POOMP!
JIM DAVIS 2-9

OOPS. I CRUNCHED JON'S ANTENNA
© 1980 PAWS, INC. All Rights Reserved.

A LITTLE MORE TO THE RIGHT, GARFIELD

GARFIELD®

WATCH THIS. I'M GOING TO SWING DOWN ON THIS VINE AND SWOOP UP JON'S CHICKEN

YANK
YANK

SWOOP!
JIM DAVIS

WHERE DID THE VINE COME FROM?
© 1980 PAWS, INC. All Rights Reserved.
2-10

GUESS WHAT, GARFIELD? THIS WEEK WE'RE GOING TO VISIT DAD AND MOM ON THE FARM
© 1980 PAWS, INC. All Rights Reserved.
2-11

YIPEE SKIP

I THINK I'LL CALL IN SICK THIS WEEK
JIM DAVIS

THERE'S ONLY ONE THING YOU HAVE TO REMEMBER WHEN WE GET TO THE FARM, GARFIELD

WATCH WHERE YOU STEP
2-12

© 1980 PAWS, INC. All Rights Reserved.
JIM DAVIS
LET ME OUT

HI, DAD
WELCOME HOME, CITY BOY

HI, MOM
EAT, EAT, EAT, EAT
© 1980 PAWS, INC. All Rights Reserved.

WELL, SHUCKY DARN AND SLOP THE CHICKENS. I THINK I'M GOING TO LIKE IT HERE
2-13
JIM DAVIS

EAT, EAT, EAT
MOM, IS THAT ALL YOU CAN SAY? "EAT, EAT, EAT"?
2-14

YOU SHOULD MEET SOME NICE GIRL, SETTLE DOWN, HAVE A FAMILY
© 1980 PAWS, INC. All Rights Reserved.
JIM DAVIS

PASS THE MASHED POTATOES
EAT, EAT, EAT

HOW'S GARFIELD ADJUSTING TO THE FARM?
JIM DAVIS 2-15

© 1980 PAWS, INC. All Rights Reserved.
OINK!

YOU MEAN, HOW'S THE FARM ADJUSTING TO GARFIELD

© 1980 PAWS, INC. All Rights Reserved.
I'M GLAD WE VISITED THE FARM, DAD
YUP

IT'S NICE TO GET AWAY FROM IT ALL
YUP

WAY, WAY, WAYYYY AWAY
JIM DAVIS 2-16

GARFIELD®

© 1980 PAWS, INC. All Rights Reserved.

2·17
JIM DAVIS

THIS WOULD BE A GOOD MORNING FOR A BRISK WALK
JIM DAVIS
2-18

© 1980 PAWS, INC. All Rights Reserved.

TO THE FOOD DISH

© 1980 PAWS, INC. All Rights Reserved.
2-19

CLACK!

LIFE WASN'T HALF AS MUCH FUN BEFORE I GOT MY YO-YO BONE
JIM DAVIS

THE CAPED AVENGER SEES AN EVIL DOG

THE CAPED AVENGER SPRINGS INTO ACTION
2-20

JIM DAVIS
THE CAPED AVENGER HURTS HIMSELF
© 1980 PAWS, INC. All Rights Reserved.

2-21
© 1980 PAWS, INC. All Rights Reserved.

SWIPE!

THANKS, GARFIELD. I HATE TO LICK STAMPS
BLUH, BLUH
JIM DAVIS

WE'RE HAVING LASAGNA FOR DINNER TONIGHT, GARFIELD
JIM DAVIS

© 1980 PAWS, INC. All Rights Reserved.
PTOOEY!

WHAT SAY I BAKE IT FIRST
WHAT SAY
2-22

I COULD USE A GOOD BACK WALK, GARFIELD
2-23

THIS IS GREAT. YOU'D MAKE SOMEONE A GOOD WIFE

NO CLAWS! NO CLAWS!
JIM DAVIS
© 1980 PAWS, INC. All Rights Reserved.

GARFIELD®

© 1980 PAWS, INC. All Rights Reserved.

IT'S NOT THE HAVING, IT'S THE GETTING
2·24
JIM DAVIS

YOU'RE TOO FAT, GARFIELD. I'M PUTTING YOU ON ANOTHER DIET
2-25

HE MAKES ME SO MAD

IF I COULD HAVE GOTTEN UP ON THAT CHAIR, I WOULD HAVE GIVEN HIM THE BEATING OF HIS LIFE
JIM DAVIS
© 1980 PAWS, INC. All Rights Reserved.

HERE'S A CARROT FOR YOUR DIET, GARFIELD. YOU KNOW WHAT TO DO WITH IT
2-26

I CERTAINLY DO
JIM DAVIS

HERE RABBIT, RABBIT, RABBIT
© 1980 PAWS, INC. All Rights Reserved.

I KNOW YOU'RE UNHAPPY, GARFIELD, BUT I WOULDN'T HAVE TO PUT YOU ON DIETS IF YOU WOULDN'T EAT SO MUCH
© 1980 PAWS, INC. All Rights Reserved.
2-27

I CAN'T HELP IT. I HAVE A GLANDULAR CONDITION...

AN OVERACTIVE MOUTH GLAND
JIM DAVIS

THIS DIET'S A REAL BUMMER. I'M GETTING WEAKER BY THE MINUTE
© 1980 PAWS, INC. All Rights Reserved.
2-28

I MUST BE GOING INTO CHOLESTEROL WITHDRAWAL

THAT'S WHEN YOU HAVE THE URGE TO MAKE A HIGHBALL OUT OF BACON GREASE
JIM DAVIS

B-R-R-R-R
2-29
© 1980 PAWS, INC. All Rights Reserved.

AWWW, POOR THING. FIRST YOU'RE ON A DIET, NOW YOU'RE FREEZING

WHERE'S YOUR BLANKET?
I ATE IT
JIM DAVIS

YOU'RE LOOKING TRIMMER, GARFIELD. I'LL TAKE YOU OFF YOUR DIET NOW
31
JIM DAVIS

© 1980 PAWS, INC. All Rights Reserved.

WHEW!
POOMP!

GARFIELD®

© 1980 PAWS, INC. All Rights Reserved.

OH NO, YOU DON'T, GARFIELD. THIS CHICKEN LEG IS MINE
3-2

LET'S HEAR IT FOR CLAWS
JIM DAVIS

GEE, I FEEL GOOD
© 1980 PAWS, INC. All Rights Reserved.
3-3

I FEEL LIKE BEING NICE TO EVERYBODY TODAY

I MUST BE COMING DOWN WITH SOMETHING
JIM DAVIS

HEH HEH
3-4

CATS LOVE TO PLAY IN GROCERY BAGS

DARN... NO GROCERIES
© 1980 PAWS, INC. All Rights Reserved.
JIM DAVIS

WHEN THE NEWSPAPER COMES EACH DAY, I TAKE THE EDITORIAL PAGE AND JON TAKES THE FUNNIES
© 1980 PAWS, INC. All Rights Reserved.
3-5

HA! HA! HA! HA!

THERE'S NO ACCOUNTING FOR SOME PEOPLE'S TASTE
JIM DAVIS

JIM DAVIS
3-6

SWIPE!

LET ME GUESS... YOU'RE HUNGRY
RIGHT ON
© 1980 PAWS, INC. All Rights Reserved.

COME ON, KITTY. SING YOUR SONG
3-7

DOO-DA, DOO-DA
JIM DAVIS
© 1980 PAWS, INC. All Rights Reserved.

OH NO!
© 1980 PAWS, INC. All Rights Reserved.
3-8

PUNT!

DON'T LAUGH. HOW WOULD YOU LIKE TO HAVE DOG DROOL ALL OVER **YOUR** TEDDY BEAR?
JIM DAVIS

GARFIELD®

© 1980 PAWS, INC. All Rights Reserved.
3-9

GRACEFUL
BLOW IT OUT YOUR EAR
JIM DAVIS

THIS LOOKS LIKE IT'S GOING TO BE A GOOD WEEK
JIM DAVIS
© 1980 PAWS, INC. All Rights Reserved.

NUTS... NUTS, NUTS, NUTS
3-10

MEYOW
© 1980 PAWS, INC. All Rights Reserved.
3-11

LISTEN TO THAT
PURRR

THE KID'S A WALKING CLICHÉ
FFFT
JIM DAVIS

WHIP!
© 1980 PAWS, INC. All Rights Reserved.
JIM DAVIS

RIP RIP RIP

AWW, HOW CUTE
3-12

GARFIELD, YOU SHOULD LEARN TO PLAY WITH NERMAL
SURE THING
HOP HOP
© 1980 PAWS, INC. All Rights Reserved.

3-13

LET ME REPHRASE THAT
DRIBBLE DRIBBLE DRIBBLE
JIM DAVIS

JIM DAVIS
3-14

HERE, NERMAL. DO SOMETHING MORE CONSTRUCTIVE WITH YOUR TIME

© 1980 PAWS, INC. All Rights Reserved.

SAY GOOD-BYE TO GARFIELD, NERMAL
SMACK
JIM DAVIS
© 1980 PAWS, INC. All Rights Reserved.

3-15

GARFIELD®

3-16

ZIP!

WHERE THERE'S A WILL...
JIM DAVIS

GARFIELD, GET YOUR LAZY BONES OUT OF BED AND COME TO BREAKFAST
GARFIELD
JIM DAVIS
© 1980 PAWS, INC. All Rights Reserved

SCRAPE
SCRAPE
SCRAPE
GARFIELD

SCRAPE
SCRAPE
SCRAPE
GARFIELD
3-17

© 1980 PAWS, INC. All Rights Reserved.
3-18

IS THAT ALL I AM TO YOU?
MERELY AN OBSTRUCTION IN THE ROAD OF LIFE
JIM DAVIS

I KNOW YOU CATS ARE INQUISITIVE BY NATURE, GARFIELD
© 1980 PAWS, INC. All Rights Reserved.

AND I KNOW THIS IS YOUR HOME AS WELL AS MINE . . .

BUT STAY OUT OF MY UNDERWEAR DRAWER!!
3-19
JIM DAVIS

COMPUTERS... EVERYTHING IS CONTROLLED BY COMPUTERS THESE DAYS
© 1980 PAWS, INC. All Rights Reserved.

THAT CHICKEN YOU ATE WAS EVEN RAISED BY A COMPUTER
3-20

burp
JIM DAVIS

LET'S GO EAT, ODIE
3-21

WHAT SAY YOU GO FORMAL

WITH A WHITE TIE AND TAIL
© 1980 PAWS, INC. All Rights Reserved.
JIM DAVIS

IT'S A MYTH THAT CATS ARE HIGH-STRUNG
© 1980 PAWS, INC. All Rights Reserved.
3-22

BARK

THERE'S A LOT OF TRUTH IN THOSE OLD MYTHS
JIM DAVIS

GARFIELD®

HAVE A FISH, GARFIELD

© 1980 PAWS, INC. All Rights Reserved.

JIM DAVIS

GULP

PTOOEY
3-23

THAT WAS AMAZING!
I HAVE NIMBLE TEETH

GUESS WHAT, GARFIELD? I'M ENTERING YOU IN A CAT SHOW
3-24
© 1980 PAWS, INC. All Rights Reserved.

THAT SHOULD BE FUN...

I'LL BE DYNAMITE IN THE SWIMSUIT COMPETITION
JIM DAVIS

YOU'LL HAVE TO TAKE A BATH BEFORE THE CAT SHOW, GARFIELD
I'LL TAKE MY CHANCES
3-25

CLEAN CATS ARE WINNING CATS

THE THINGS I DO FOR STARDOM
© 1980 PAWS, INC. All Rights Reserved.
JIM DAVIS

NOW LET'S FLUFF YOU UP
3-26

RRRRRR

© 1980 PAWS, INC. All Rights Reserved.
JIM DAVIS

WE NEED A GIMMICK FOR THE CAT SHOW, GARFIELD, SOMETHING TO MAKE THE JUDGE NOTICE YOU
3-27

THIS SHOULD DO IT

IT'S A SAD STATE OF AFFAIRS WHEN A PET OWNER STOOPS TO HUMILIATING A CAT
JIM DAVIS
© 1980 PAWS, INC. All Rights Reserved.

THEY'LL PROBABLY WANT YOU TO DO TRICKS AT THE CAT SHOW, GARFIELD. SO HOP THROUGH THIS HOOP

3-28

I COULD JUST CRY
JIM DAVIS
© 1980 PAWS, INC. All Rights Reserved.

HURRY UP, GARFIELD! TIME TO LEAVE FOR THE CAT SHOW
GRRR
ROWR
© 1980 PAWS, INC. All Rights Reserved.
3-29

YIP! ROWR! FFT!

I COULD JUST CRY
JIM DAVIS

GARFIELD®

THIS IS IT, GARFIELD. YOUR FIRST CAT SHOW

WHERE DO I PUT MY CAT ?
PUT HIM HERE
CAT SHOW
JIM DAVIS 3-30

CAT SHOW
© 1980 PAWS, INC. All Rights Reserved.

how
to draw
Garfield

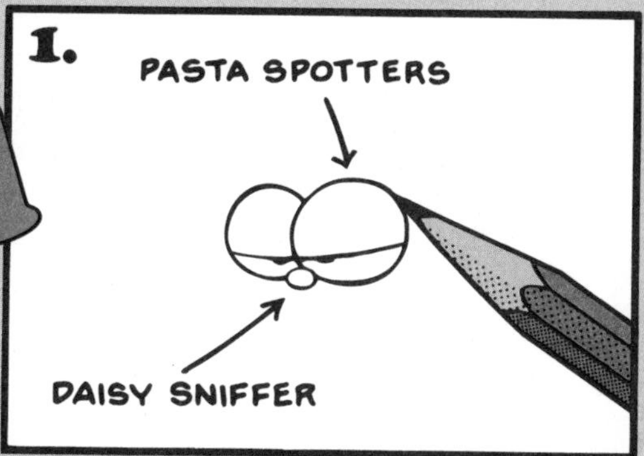
1.
PASTA SPOTTERS
DAISY SNIFFER

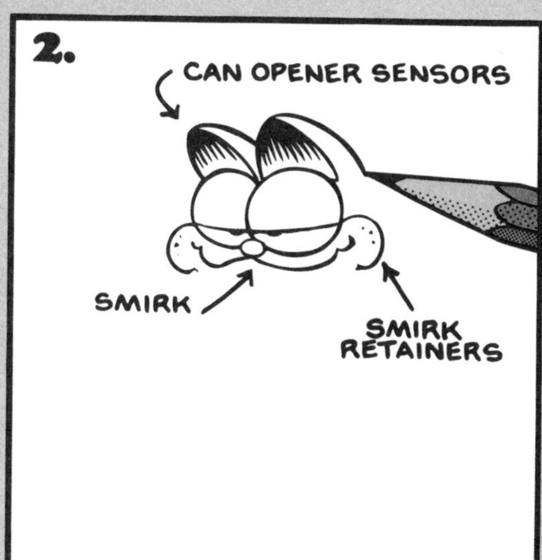
2.
CAN OPENER SENSORS
SMIRK
SMIRK RETAINERS

3.
STROKING SURFACE
LASAGNA STORAGE UNITS
TWITCHER

4.
HAIR BALL CATCHER
DIRT DRAGGER
CHAIR SHREDDERS

5.
NOT JUST ANOTHER PRETTY FACE
STRIPES
NOW ADD THE PERSONALITY
JIM DAVIS

Garfield
Up Close and Personal

Q: What is your favorite sport?
A: *Each morning, before breakfast, I like to take a good, brisk nap.*

Q: Where did you get your nasty temper, and why are you so cynical?
A: *Step a little closer and ask that.*

Q: Describe your relationship with Jon, Odie, Pooky, and Nermal.
A: *Someone to abuse, someone to pound on, someone to confide in, and no comment.*

Q: Why did you call your most recent book *GARFIELD Bigger Than Life*?
A: *I didn't name the book, actually. I have the distinct feeling it is some kind of slur on my size. The book was named by my late editor.*

Q: How much money did you get for this book?
A: *Heavens to Betsy, I'm just a cat. That sort of thing doesn't concern me. Ask my agent.*

Q: Now that you are a success, do you give yourself your own baths?
A: *No, I've hired a cat to take baths for me.*

Q: Are you a prima donna?
A: *Not really.*

Q: Is there anyone with whom you would like to share the credit for your success?
A: *Not really.*